Kauffman's

MANUAL OF RIDING SAFETY

Photographs by Walter Bredel

Drawings by Werner Rentsch

Kauffman's

MANUAL OF RIDING SAFETY

BY SANDRA KAUFFMAN

Clarkson N. Potter, Inc. / *Publishers* NEW YORK

DISTRIBUTED BY CROWN PUBLISHERS, INC.

Published simultaneously in Canada by General Publishing Company Limited
First edition
Printed in the United States of America

Library of Congress Cataloging in Publication Data

Kauffman, Sandra.
      Kauffman's manual of riding safety.

      1. Horsemanship—Safety measures.   I. Title.
II. Title: Manual of riding safety.
SF309.K33 1977   798'.23'025   77-28729

ISBN 0-517-53293-X

To my husband,
Charles Kauffman,
with love and
admiration

Acknowledgments

This book would not have been possible without the help and support of several rare people. I am deeply indebted to John A. Wilson, who knows everything there is to know about horses and who answered my interminable questions with infinite patience, kindness, and tact.

To Jill and Walter Bredel of Meadowbrook Riding Farm, who graciously provided the riders, horses, and settings for the photographs; to Dr. Ivan Safonoff, who was so generous with his time and advice; to my mother, Celia Breslerman, who loved and cared for my children while this work was in progress; and to my daughters, Alexandra and Nicole, for their sweetness and good humor throughout.

CONTENTS

INTRODUCTION

Horseback riding is one of the fastest growing sports in the world today. In the United States alone, more than 12½ million horses are kept and ridden purely for pleasure. The animal who was once our railroad and our motorcar, our fire engine, our mail wagon and our plow, is now the boon companion of our leisure, and the expression "worked like a horse" is as obsolete as the Pony Express.

When we talk about a horse's "work" today, we mean the exercise needed to keep him healthy and fit. Fit to show, to compete, or to simply accompany us on a pleasant trail ride.

Keeping him healthy and fit, however, is no easy task. His coat must be clipped, his diet balanced, his environment monitored. His feet must be picked out and his stall mucked out. He must be inoculated against disease and rid of all the parasites eager to reside in his warm, friendly body. Besides being expensive, horsekeeping is hard work. Why, then, is it so popular?

One answer is that horses satisfy our yearning for a more natural way of life. They remind us of a time when man lived closer to the earth and to the other creatures of the earth, a time when it was still possible to carve one's destiny out of the wilderness. In this age of mechanization and environmental disaster, riding is a return to basics. It brings us out into fresh air and wholesome surroundings and provides an excellent outlet for nervous tension. Although it uses most of our body's muscles, it is not strenuous, it is easy to learn, and it can be enjoyed at almost any age. Moreover, it is an emotional experience. Like love, it requires personal involvement with another living creature and, for this reason, affects us more deeply than mere sport. Riding is a partnership between two beings who act as one, and it demands perfect communication so that each learns to anticipate the other's actions, learns, almost, to read the other's mind.

Ironically, this partnership that makes riding so satisfying can make it dangerous as well. Both parties are alive and, therefore, unpredictable. What happens when they do not act as one? What happens when communication fails and each acts independently of the other? Riding may be exciting, but is it safe? What exactly do you risk when you saddle this beautiful, but immensely powerful, animal?

It is the purpose of this book to show that you need not risk anything at all if you and your horse have been properly trained. For each of you, there is a right way of doing things and a wrong way. The wrong way threatens your safety; the right way ensures it.

In the following pages, we have set down the right way and explained exactly why it *is* right. We feel that, without knowing the reasons behind the rules, you would find a list of do's and don'ts extremely arbitrary. The rules for horsemen, however, are anything but arbitrary. Each has a definite purpose, and each arises out of the nature and psychology of the horse. Once you understand that nature, you will understand why some methods are safe and others dangerous. You will see how greatly your own behavior affects your horse, and how much of your safety lies in your own hands. Hopefully, you will ride "by the book" from then on and assure yourself a long and healthy life on horseback.

RIDING CLOTHES

When you ride, you use your body to communicate with your horse and, in order to convey your instructions properly, you must be able to move freely. Anything that restrains or inhibits you will mar your performance and threaten your safety.

Correct riding clothes are essential to your well-being. By allowing your body to move without strain or discomfort, they increase its efficiency and reduce the chance of accident. When an accident does occur, they dull the impact and, in many cases, prevent tragedy. In our discussion, we will concentrate on the protective aspect of riding wear, rather than on the dress requirements of horse show competition.*

HEADWEAR

The most valuable piece of equipment you will ever own is a hard, protective safety cap. If you fall from your horse or are thrown, if your head hits a rock or if you are stepped on, its strong outer shell and interior padding can save your life. Never, *never* ride without it. And never underestimate its importance. Use it the way you use your safety belt in an automobile: No matter how short a distance you are going, no matter how good a rider you are, *put it on!* Today's most effective caps are made with adjustable leather chin straps and harnesses that will keep the cap on your head if you fall or get hit. However, harnesses may also be purchased separately and mounted on standard hunt caps.

Ideally, a safety hat should have a hard outer shell, a well-padded interior, a chin strap and harness, web suspension, and a flexible brim that will pop up when you fall, rather than come down on your nose and break it. Although no one cap at present is one hundred percent safe, the regulation jockey cap and several adaptations of hunt caps do come close, and are the only riding hats that provide any true protection. Traditional hunt caps, hunt derbies, saddle seat derbies, and toppers provide practically no protection, and the Western riding hat, though a requisite in Western classes, is purely decorative.

A word about hair: If yours is long, tie it back, roll it into a bun, or wear a net under your cap. Flying hair is always bad form, but more important than that, it gets into your eyes and obstructs your vision.

---

*For a complete rundown on correct show attire, consult the rules book of the American Horse Shows Association, 598 Madison Avenue, New York, N.Y. 10022. A small fee will get you the book plus membership in the Association.

FOOTWEAR

From a safety standpoint, proper footwear is almost as important to a rider as proper headwear. The right shoes or boots will protect you in the stable as well as on the horse; the wrong ones can get you into serious trouble.

While a good pair of English or Western riding boots should be the goal of every serious rider, there are less expensive substitutes for beginners and growing children. Provided they have a heel and a hard sole, you can ride in work boots, hiking boots, and even ordinary street boots (or shoes). Rubber riding boots are also appropriate. However, shoes without heels, like sneakers and moccasins, are dangerous because they allow your feet to slip all the way through the stirrup irons. If you fall from your horse while one of your feet is trapped in an iron, you will be dragged along the ground. A rider must always be able to extract his feet from the stirrups without difficulty, and any shoe or piece of equipment that prevents him from doing so is taboo. This includes Vibram-soled boots (boots with deeply grooved soles) and stirrup irons that are too tight or too loose. (The former will lock your feet in; the latter will end up around your ankles.) Also taboo, but for another reason, are soft shoes with soft soles, like sandals, moccasins, and tennis sneakers. These can be easily penetrated and ripped open by nails, rocks, and other loose-lying debris in and around barns, and will not protect your feet if you are stepped on by a horse.

ENGLISH AND WESTERN RIDING BOOTS

The tall English riding boot is traditionally worn with breeches and, despite its good looks, is designed strictly for protection. It keeps the stirrup leathers from rubbing and burning the rider's legs and prevents the metal stirrups from hurting his ankles. However, in order to be effective, boots must fit properly. When you purchase an English boot, make sure it just clears the bend in your leg, since it will drop about three-quarters of an inch on wearing. Also make sure that it fits closely at the top and at the calf. Two of your fingers should fit comfortably into the top, with no excessive play.

Most English boots are made with straps on the inside to keep breeches from riding up and forming uncomfortable wrinkles. Called *garter straps*, these should be buckled around your leg, with the buckle on the outside and the loose end of the strap pointing to the rear.

English boots also feature inside loops called *boot pulls*, which enable the rider to insert boot hooks. To put your boots on properly, pull your socks up over the bottom of your breeches so the breeches don't catch on the edge of the boots. Insert your boot hooks in the boot pulls and put your foot into the boot as far as it will go. Then, stand up and pull gently on the boot hooks as you push your foot downward. Never pull too hard on the hooks or you will rip the pulls.

Like its English counterpart, the tall Western riding boot protects its wearer from leather burns and metal bruises. However, unlike its English cousin, it features a high heel and a pointed toe, two definite safety pluses. The pointed toe makes it easy for the rider to find his stirrups once he is in the saddle; the high heel makes it difficult for the stirrups to slip over the rider's legs and trap them.

The Western boot also comes with loops that make it easy to pull on, but it is worn under, rather than over, Western riding pants.

SPURS

These are useful in the saddle but dangerous on the ground. Take them off as soon as you finish your ride. If you walk in them, they are apt to trip you.

RIDING PANTS

Good riding pants should be neat, soft, and well fitted: neat, so that buttons, belts, and straps do not snag on equipment or get hooked over saddle horns; soft and well fitted, so that you are not chafed or uncomfortable. Although pants should fit snugly, they should never be tight enough to cut you in the crotch or rub your legs.

The type of pants you choose will be determined by your age, budget, and style of riding. Jodhpurs, breeches, street slacks, and jeans are all acceptable for pleasure riding, although new jeans must be washed several times before wearing, to prevent chafing. Unless *all* the sizing is removed, the fabric will rub your skin raw.

Never ride in shorts or in any other garment that does not cover your legs completely. Unless you ride bareback, the saddle leathers will burn you badly.

OTHER CLOTHING

Hacking jackets, hunt coats, raincoats, and all other coats made specifically for riders are vented in the back to permit freedom of movement around the hips. If you ride in any other type of coat, make sure it allows you the same freedom and does not constrict you in any way.

Riding gloves protect your hands both on and off the horse and should be worn to ward off stable germs and prevent splinters, cuts, and rope burns. String gloves will give you the best grip, especially in wet weather, but most gloves are acceptable, provided they give you contact with the reins and allow your fingers to move freely. Mittens are unacceptable.

HOW TO CLEAN AND CARE FOR RIDING CLOTHES

Riding clothes take more of a beating and get dirtier than almost any other specialized garments. Here are some suggestions for cleaning them.

VELVET CAPS

To remove lint and surface soil, rub your cap with strips of Scotch tape. Then, steam it over a kettle to loosen dirt and go over it lightly with a medium-bristle brush.

LEATHER BOOTS

Sweat from the horse will discolor leather boots. Immediately after riding, go over them with saddle soap and a damp cloth. Then put them on boot trees to air out.

When you polish them, remember that leather must breathe, so use a cream polish, never one that will seal the pores. Store your boots only in a cool, dry place. Keep them away from dampness. If you are caught in a rainstorm, never try to quick-dry them by placing them near heat, since heat will cause them to crack. Allow them to dry naturally, then apply a leather conditioner such as Lexol or Murphy's Oil Soap.

BREECHES

Launder your breeches properly by following these directions:

1. Remove all surface dirt and mud with a clean, soft-bristle clothes brush.
2. Wet the breeches thoroughly in lukewarm water and wash them with a mild detergent. If you wash them by machine, set the wash cycle at "Gentle" or "Slow." Avoid extreme agitation. If you wash them by hand, avoid excessive rubbing.
3. Rinse the breeches thoroughly in cold water and allow them to dry slowly and naturally. Never put them in an electric dryer or hang them out in the sun. While they are still damp, lay them on a table and pull them lengthwise so they resume their natural shape. Don't be upset if they seem to have shrunk: They will stretch out to their original size when you put them on.
4. Press the breeches with a warm, *never* hot, iron.

RIDING JACKETS

Most riding jackets are not as tightly woven as riding pants and need to be dry cleaned. However, a jacket that is only slightly soiled can be freshened up with a clean, stiff-bristle clothes brush, a damp sponge, and a mild detergent. Use one teaspoon of detergent to one pint of water and dampen only the surface of the garment, not the lining.

RUBBER RAINCOATS

Always wash your raincoat by hand in lukewarm water, then lay it on a table and brush it clean. Allow it to dry naturally; never put it in an electric dryer.

GLOVES

All leather gloves, with the exception of suede, can be laundered. Put them on your hands as if you were going to wear them, and wash them with water and a mild soap. Then, rinse them thoroughly and apply saddle soap. When you have wiped off the excess, gently remove the gloves from your hands and allow them to dry.

To launder string gloves, soak them in lukewarm, sudsy water for an hour. Never rub them. After rinsing, put them on your hands for a few minutes and allow them to regain their natural shape.

HOW TO CLEAN
AND CARE
FOR TACK

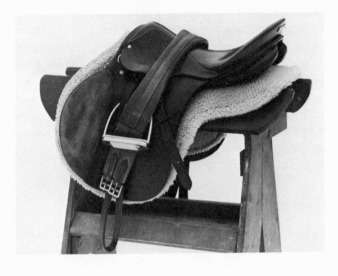

Imagine what would happen if your girth broke while you were riding—or if one of your bridle rings snapped. In the first instance, your saddle would begin to slide, and you would lose the security of your seat. In the second, you would lose control of your horse's mouth and would not be able to stop him when you chose.

Clearly, a rider's safety depends as much on his tack as it does on his riding ability. To make sure your equipment does not let you down when you need it most, learn to care for it properly and keep it in good condition.

To prevent dirt, mud, saliva, and sweat from building up and decaying materials, you must clean your tack after every ride. If you ride frequently, you must also give it a special cleaning at least once a week. This means you must take all the pieces apart and clean under folds and other hard-to-reach areas. Open the reins, the cheeks, the stirrup leathers. Go underneath the saddle panels. Take apart the bridle and pay particular attention to the leather around the bit. This is constantly being wetted and is especially vulnerable to drying and cracking. Pay particular attention, too, to any leather that is folded over, or any bit of tack that is covered by another material—these are the pieces most frequently overlooked.

TO CLEAN LEATHER

To clean leather, you will need the following items:

- A leather conditioner, to replace natural oils that dry out of the skin. The two most popular are Lexol and Neats-foot Oil.
- Saddle soap, to replenish oils and also to clean.
- Several sponges.
- A suede brush, if your saddle is made of suede or doeskin or if it has suede knee rolls.

RULES FOR CLEANING LEATHER

1. Wash away all mud, dirt, grass, saliva, and sweat with a damp sponge. Pay particular attention to areas that have touched the horse, since these are bound to be sweatier than others.
2. Apply saddle soap to a damp sponge or a soft cloth and rub it thoroughly into the leather. Wipe off any excess.
3. Treat leather with a leather conditioner at least once a month or after every six or seven rides.

SPECIAL PRECAUTIONS

Condition all your leather equipment immediately after purchase. Conditioning protects leather, keeps it supple, and makes it last longer.

Never saturate leather with any liquid—including water. Cloths and sponges used in cleaning should be damp, not soaking wet. After cleaning or conditioning, leather should always be wiped dry.

Be especially careful when washing around stitching—if the threads get too wet, they will eventually dry up and crack.

Never use heavy oils on leather—they make the skin weak and spongy and also come off on your clothes.

Allow leather to darken gradually. Don't use heavy stains— they seep into the pores and make the skin hard and cakey.

Store all your leather equipment in a cool, dry place. If you expose it to cold or to direct sunlight for long periods of time, it will dry out and crack.

Remember that the under panels of your saddle rest on the horse's back and will always be sweaty after use. Allow the panels to dry out by storing your saddle on a rack that permits air to circulate freely around it.

A WORD ABOUT YOUR SADDLE PAD

After every ride, go over it with a damp, stiff brush to remove all traces of sweat, and hang it out to dry. When you wash it, do so in clear water and dry it thoroughly before you put it back on your horse.

TO CLEAN METAL

To clean metal you will need:

- Clean, clear water
- A soft cloth
- Metal polish
- Steel wool

RULES FOR CLEANING METAL

1. Wash all your metal equipment—bits, stirrups, hardware, etc.—with clear water (and soap or detergent if necessary) and wipe it dry.

2. Never rub metal with steel wool or scrape it with sharp instruments. Such materials create rough surfaces and jagged edges that will cut and scratch your horse. However, you may use steel wool on stirrup *treads* since these do not touch the horse's body, are difficult to clean, and are slippery when dirty.
3. After your equipment is completely cleaned and dried, buff it thoroughly with a soft cloth. If you use metal polish, make sure it contains no ingredient that may be poisonous, or otherwise harmful, to your horse. Bits are best left unpolished since horses generally find the taste of the polish objectionable.

GENERAL RULES FOR CLEANING TACK

Don't allow residues of soaps, polishes, cleansers, or conditioners to build up on your equipment. Make sure all materials used in cleaning are either completely rubbed into your tack or wiped off it.

Before you try any new product, check its ingredients, and don't use any products your horse may be allergic to.

Finally, when cleaning your tack, always do the best job you possibly can. If you do slipshod work or take shortcuts, you only endanger yourself.

Caution: Even well-cared-for tack wears out eventually. Before every ride, make sure you examine all your equipment for cracks, tears, weak spots, and loose hardware. If you find any defective parts, do not use the equipment until those parts have been replaced.

HANDLING
HORSES
SAFELY

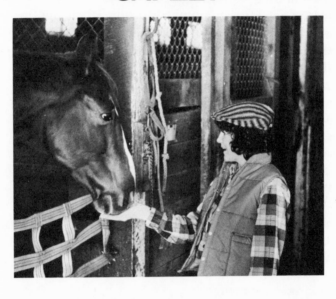

For thousands of years, the horse has considered man his teacher and his ally. Far from the herd and the environment of his ancestors, he looks to man for leadership and control and is a cooperative and eager pupil. Yet the horse has never forgotten that he was once a hunted animal. Despite years of domestication, he is still a timid creature who frightens easily and strikes out in self-defense whenever he is startled or upset. To handle him safely, you must overcome his fears and build up his confidence in himself and in you. You must maintain a firm hand and an even temper, and you must behave in a confident and relaxed manner whenever you are with him. If *you* are comfortable and assured, chances are he will be too. On the

14

other hand, if you are anxious and insecure, he will pick up your anxiety, behave badly and threaten your safety. Like most animals, the horse tends to assume the characteristics of his caretakers, and that is why a confident handler is so important to his performance and his state of mind.

Confidence being the key, the obvious questions are: Where does it come from, and how do you get it?

The best source of confidence is knowledge. When you understand the horse's nature and his needs, when you know how to approach and handle him properly, when you are trained by an accredited instructor and taught how to behave in the saddle, you will not be timid and fearful. You will have no reason to be. Your training will give you weapons to combat your anxiety. In learning to anticipate and deal with dangerous situations and also to prevent them, in learning that you are in control of events, not at their mercy, you are sure to develop all the confidence you need to handle your horse properly.

Confidence, however, never implies lack of caution. When dealing with horses, you must never relax your guard at any time. The majority of accidents are caused by simple carelessness (or neglect) on the part of the very people who ought to know better. While fear will always work against you, the right amount of caution can save your life and limbs.

The parts of a horse

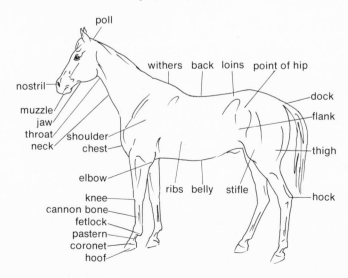

HOW TO APPROACH A HORSE

Since a horse is easily startled by strange (to him) sounds, sudden movements, and loud noises, do not barge in on him or sneak up on him, because he may kick with his hind legs or run away. These are his favorite methods of self-defense, and he employs them instinctively. To keep him from employing them on you, approach him slowly and speak softly to him before you do. By speaking, you make him aware of your presence and also make sure he is awake. Horses often sleep standing up, and if you surprise one in that condition, you can trigger an equine explosion.

Once you have spoken, approach your horse from the side (preferably the left side), never from the front or rear. If you approach from the front, he will have to throw back his head or back away from you in order to get you in focus. This is because his eyes, like the eyes of all hunted animals, are set on the sides of his head (the hunters have front-set eyes), and he cannot see directly in front of him. (Remember this when you pet him and don't go for his nose—stroke his neck or shoulder instead.) He can, however, see very well from the side and can even see both left and right at the same time.

You can approach your horse from the side even if he is in a straight stall. Open the chain or rope behind him, enter from the left, and walk toward him at an angle. Always walk beyond the

How to feed a horse a treat

reach of his heels, and never step over his tie rope or duck under it. If he is in a box stall, train him to come to you at the door.

If you want to offer him a carrot, a piece of apple, or some other treat, place it in the palm of your hand and keep your hand absolutely flat when you extend it to him. If your fingers or your thumb are poking up, he can easily mistake them for another offering.

GROOMING

If you are lucky enough to own your own horse, chances are you will want to take an active part in his daily care. From a safety standpoint, you would be very wise to do so. Caring for a horse is one of the best ways to get to know him, and the more you know about the horse you ride, the safer your ride will be.

Similarly, the horse who is familiar with his rider, who knows him to be an able and dependable caretaker, is more apt to trust him in the saddle, more apt to perform what is expected of him. By working together day after day, horse and rider establish a bond of sympathy and understanding that makes communication easier and riding more satisfying.

WHAT IS THE PURPOSE OF GROOMING?

Grooming cleans the horse and removes wastes that give rise to parasites and skin disease. It also conditions the horse, keeps his muscles toned, and improves his circulation.

HOW OFTEN SHOULD A HORSE BE GROOMED?

In order to stay well and maintain a healthy appearance, a horse needs to be groomed at least once a day. A stabled horse should receive a light grooming before his exercise and a thorough one after it. A horse at grass should receive a light grooming only so he can keep the natural oils in his coat that protect him against dampness and cold. However, if he is saddled, his back and girth area should be thoroughly cleaned.

By establishing a regular daily routine in the stable, you can help your horse overcome many of his natural fears. A creature of habit, he thrives on a fixed schedule and loves having each thing done at the same time every day. He also loves the company of his own kind, and if you work on him within sight or hearing distance of other horses, he will be easier to handle and far less anxious.

WHAT DO YOU USE TO GROOM A HORSE?

A grooming kit should contain the following items:

- Dandy brush: a brush with long, stiff hairs used to remove dirt and mud. (It is usually the only brush used on a horse at grass.)

Grooming implements

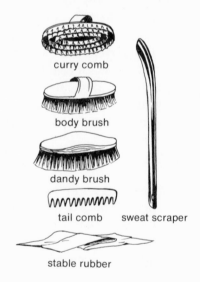

curry comb

body brush

dandy brush

tail comb　　sweat scraper

stable rubber

- Body brush: a soft, short-haired brush with a strap that goes over the hand. Used to groom the coat of a stabled horse, and to brush out his mane and tail.
- Curry comb: usually a metal comb with short teeth used to clean the dandy brush and the body brush. When made of rubber, it is also used on the horse's neck and body to remove dirt, mud, and loose hair.
- Hoof pick: a metal hook used for cleaning out the horse's feet.

- Body sponge: a large sponge used to wash the horse's body.
- Muzzle sponge: a small sponge for washing the horse's eyes, nostrils, and mouth.
- Dock sponge: a small sponge for washing the horse's rectal area.
- Sweat scraper: a metal or plastic blade used for removing sweat and water after washing and sponging.
- Water brush: a long brush with soft bristles that is dampened to smooth down the mane and tail.
- Mane-and-tail comb: a metal close-toothed comb about six inches long.
- Stable rubber: a linen cloth used to give a final polish to the horse after grooming.

HOW DO YOU GROOM A HORSE?

You groom a horse primarily by brushing, combing, and sponging him with the implements described above. This method of cleaning is safer and more effective than washing since it gives the horse the conditioning and muscle tone he needs without wetting and chilling his body and subjecting him to possible infection.

In the following pages, we will outline the grooming procedure and tell you what precautions to take, but will not instruct you in the actual method. For your horse's protection and your own, this is best learned from a qualified teacher who can demonstrate on a living animal. In going over your horse from head to toe, you will be working close to him and dealing with highly sensitive areas of his body that become sensitized even further when infected or sore. Unless you know exactly what you are doing, you can get yourself into serious trouble. An inexperienced rider, armed only with grooming kit and instruction manual, works at his own risk.

THE GROOMING PROCEDURE

1. Before starting, assemble all your grooming tools in one place, so you won't irritate your horse by constantly running off to retrieve missing items. Check to make sure your tools are clean and in good condition. Keep them ac-

cessible when working, and don't drop them on the floor to be stepped on and tripped over.

2. Fasten your horse to a ring in his stall, to a ring or post outdoors, or to a cross-tie in the stable aisle. If another horse is in the aisle, don't pass or squeeze by unless you know the two horses are absolutely compatible. Horses may love the company of their own kind, but they have their likes and dislikes just as people do, and confrontations of any sort are always risky.

3. To groom your horse, go over him thoroughly and remove all dried sweat, manure, and caked-on mud. Be especially sure to clean under the tail and around the dock (rectal area). Pick the debris out of the feet and untangle all matted hair. Dirt that won't come out with brushing can be washed out with soap, warm water, and a sponge. However, before you use even a modicum of water on a horse, make sure he is not in a draft.

4. Learn to clean the horse's feet correctly so you don't injure them in any way. Clean them in the same order every time so the horse will get used to the routine and lift them automatically. Remember that they are crucial to

To clean a horse's foot with a hoof pick, stroke away from your body toward the horse's toe.

his well-being. Never lift them up too high or carry them back too far. You must preserve the horse's balance and your own as well. If you accidentally slip or stumble, the horse may become frightened and injure you unintentionally.

5. While working on your horse, speak softly to him and tell him exactly what you are going to do before you do it. Never grab him unexpectedly or cause him unnecessary pain. If you plan to groom him with electric clippers, make sure the noise does not frighten him. Let him hear them from a distance before you begin clipping. Remember that his feet are his first line of defense. Hurt him or startle him, and he will retaliate by kicking.

6. When working on your horse, examine him closely for cuts, sores, or bruises. Be on the lookout for any sign of illness or infection. If your horse is sick, he will still need to be groomed, though not quite as vigorously. Twice a day is recommended, as much for the company it affords the horse as for his treatment and conditioning.

RULES FOR WORKING AROUND HORSES

Always wear boots or hard shoes in a stable or barnyard. If a horse steps on your foot, soft shoes like moccasins or tennis sneakers will not dull the pain. Nor will they protect you from pebbles, rocks, and other loose-lying debris. Bare feet, of course, are an invitation to disaster.

Always enter a stable calmly and quietly. Never rush in or make loud noises. If another horse is being groomed on cross-ties, you may frighten him and cause him to hurt his handler.

To prevent a horse from kicking or stepping on you, stay outside the range of his heels whenever possible. When grooming, however, work as close to his body as you can so that, if he does kick, he will push you away from him, and you will not receive the full impact of the blow.

It is also important to work where the horse can see you so that he does not become anxious. Work from a position as near his shoulder as possible. Never stand behind him. Even when grooming his tail, stand at his side (near the point of the buttock) and pull the tail gently toward you.

Never allow children to walk between a horse's legs or walk underneath the horse to demonstrate how gentle he is. That "gentle" horse may surprise you!

Never tease a horse. This is important for several reasons. First, he may develop dangerous habits that are not easily broken. And second, he may not be ready to stop playing when you are, or indeed realize you are playing! If your horse does develop bad habits, he becomes a serious threat to you and to others who are not aware of them.

LEADING THE HORSE

While everyone knows "you can lead a horse to water, etc.," not everyone knows the right—or safe—way to do it. If you plan to lead a horse, to water or anywhere else, this is the correct procedure.

GETTING THE HORSE READY

Pass a halter over the horse's head (noseband first), keeping the rope, or lead shank, on the left side. If the horse is haltered and tied when you arrive, grasp the lead shank just below the halter with your right hand. Untie the horse and hold him in place for a few moments so he doesn't get into the habit of running off as soon as he is loose. Carry the excess shank folded in your left hand so you don't trip over it.

If the horse is wearing a bridle and not a halter, pull the reins forward over his head and hold them in your right hand just below the bit. Again, carry the excess shank folded in your left hand. If the horse is wearing a double bridle (which has a curved bit and a bridoon), knot the bit reins *on* the neck or fasten them under the stirrups and lead by the bridoon. Always hold reins and lead shanks close under the horse's chin so if he jumps unexpectedly, you will be pushed away from him and out of his path. Never loop reins or lead shanks around your fingers, wrist, or body. If the horse suddenly moves off, you will lose your hold on him and also run the risk of snapping your wrist or fingers. A knot at the end of the shank will give you a better grip on it in times of stress.

LEAVING THE STALL

Stabled horses are housed in box stalls or straight stalls. The box stall is larger and allows the horse to move around. The straight stall does not. If your horse is in a box stall, you will have enough room to turn him toward the door and lead him out of it. If he is in a straight stall, you will have to *back* him out. In either case, you will lead from the left side and walk slowly and deliberately to avoid slips, knocks, and bumps.

LEADING THE HORSE

A horse is always liveliest when he knows he is going out. For maximum control, lead him on a short shank. Too much rope can entangle him or encourage him to play dangerous games. Keep him out of trouble by making him walk beside you at all times. Keep his head in line with your own and never allow him to run in front of you or drag behind.

Never give your horse the opportunity to crowd you or step on you. Make him look and walk straight ahead and nudge him gently in the neck with your elbow if he veers.

Always precede him through gates, doors, and other narrow openings. After you have passed through, step quickly to one side, so he can enter without being jostled. Never try to squeeze through together.

If the horse you are leading is wearing a saddle, run up the stirrups so they will not get caught on protruding objects. *Running up* stirrups means sliding them up to the spring bar under

A stirrup that has been run up

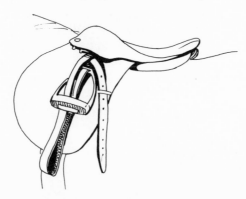

The safe way to lead a horse

the leathers and holding them in place by passing the loop ends through the irons.

Avoid leading your horse past another horse in close quarters unless you know the two animals are compatible. If you have any doubts, wait until the other horse is out of the way.

Avoid overly long lead ropes that can entangle you and your horse. When you use a lariat or a lunge line, stay clear of the coils.

Avoid catching your hands and fingers in halter and bridle hardware. Straps and leathers contain a maze of metal rings, snaps, loops, and bits that can easily trap the unwary handler.

WHAT TO DO IF YOUR HORSE WON'T MOVE

The safest way to deal with a stubborn horse is to catch him off guard with a surprise maneuver. If he won't walk, turn his head to one side and try leading him to the left or right instead of straight ahead. This change of direction will usually be enough to divert his attention from whatever is troubling him and propel him into action again. Under no circumstances should you get in front of a horse and try to pull him along. The use of force or brute strength on an animal many times your size and weight is useless as well as dangerous.

BRIDLES AND BRIDLING

Fighting a daily battle over a simple routine can be a nightmare for horse and rider alike. Yet such nightmares are bound to occur when a handler disregards his horse's feelings, ignores his problems, and acts in a thoughtless, inconsiderate manner. Horses need sympathy and understanding, just as people do. And in most instances, it takes only a little consideration to prevent a great deal of misery. Bridling, often a traumatic experience for a horse, is a good case in point.

The parts of a snaffle bridle

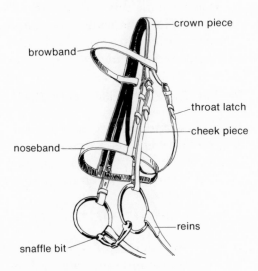

The parts of a double bridle

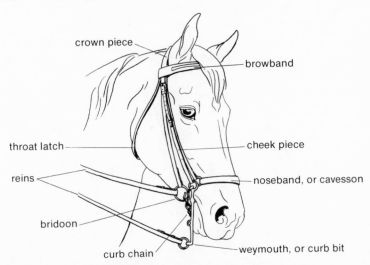

When you insert a metal bit into a horse's mouth, you are asking him to accept a foreign object and, just possibly, a painful one. Whether he accepts it readily or reacts violently depends largely on your approach. Hurt or frighten him, and you can expect a long, hard battle. Work carefully, respect his fears, and you will leave no physical or psychological scars to wreak havoc on your daily rounds.

To make your job easier and safer, be consistent. Your horse learns by rote, and constant repetition teaches him what to expect of you. If you follow the same procedure and take the same steps in the same order whenever you bridle him, you will increase his confidence in you and give him a sense of security.

WHERE DO YOU BRIDLE A HORSE?

A horse may be bridled and saddled wherever he is groomed. However, if you have a nervous animal, give him plenty of space. Don't bridle him in close quarters and don't bridle *any* horse when his head is down or when he is eating.

THE PROPER FIT OF A BRIDLE

All horses have different degrees of sensitivity in the mouth, and you will have to experiment until you find the correct type of bit for your particular horse. However, the trouble is well taken, because the more comfortable your horse is, the better he will perform and the more control you will have over him.

Try to make bridling as painless as possible for your horse by

The proper fit of a bit

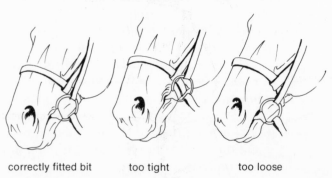

correctly fitted bit   too tight   too loose

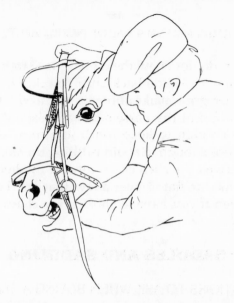

How to insert a bit into a horse's mouth

being reasonably sure that the bit will fit him. Hold it under his jaw, parallel to its normal position in his mouth, and measure it with your eye. If a bit is too narrow, it will pinch the skin; if too wide, it will bruise it; if too loose, the horse will manipulate it with his tongue.

HOW TO BRIDLE A HORSE

Stand in close behind the left side of the horse's head, and slip the bridle reins over his neck so he cannot get away from you. If he throws his head or strikes to avoid the bridle, your position behind his head will protect your own.

Feel the bit to make sure it is neither too hot (from the sun) nor too cold. Then hold it in your left hand and guide it into the horse's mouth while holding the crown of the bridle above his head with your right hand. If the horse does not open his mouth to receive the bit, insert your left thumb into the corner of his mouth and he will usually oblige.

When guiding the bit into the horse's mouth, handle it with care—never allow it to bang against the horse's teeth.

Use caution whenever you handle the horse's ears. When placing the bridle on his head, pass the crown piece first over one ear, then the other.

Before you ride, adjust the bridle so that it fits the horse properly. First, do not allow the crown piece to ride up against the horse's ears or to slide back on his neck. Do not make the throat latch too tight—make sure you can fit the width of your hand between it and the horse's throat. Make sure the browband is tight enough to keep the bridle from slipping backwards, and loose enough to avoid rubbing the horse's head and ears. Finally, twist the curb chain toward the horse's body, so that all the links lie flat. Never allow that last link to dangle. Hook it on even if you have to shorten the chain.

SADDLES AND SADDLING

QUESTIONS TO ASK WHEN BUYING A SADDLE

Is the Saddle Sound?

A saddle is constructed around a wooden frame called a tree. This tree is reinforced with metal on its underside and at its head and gullet, and is then webbed and padded. If it is broken in any way, the saddle itself can become a lethal instrument. If the pommel is cracked, the saddle will press on the horse's withers and cause cuts, abrasions, and pain. If the wood on the side is cracked, the saddle will ride on the horse's backbone and cause him grave injury. A horse that is jumped with such a saddle can easily have his back broken.

There are two ways you can test your saddle for a broken tree:

The parts of an English saddle

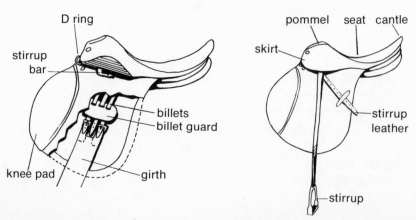

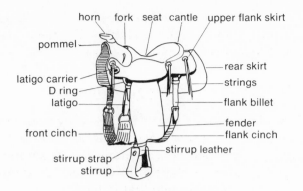

The parts of a Western saddle

1. Pick up the saddle by the pommel and, holding the cantle against your body, push the saddle toward you, causing strain. A slight amount of flexibility is normal; more than that is suspicious and needs to be investigated.
2. Turn the saddle upside down and lay it across a sawhorse. Push it slightly and check under the padding for unusual amounts of flexibility.

THE HORIZONTAL TEST

Place a hand on either side of the pommel and, holding the cantle against your body, push the sides of the saddle toward each other, then pull them back. If this push-pull motion causes any flexibility at all, the pommel is probably cracked.

Riding with a broken saddle is a good way to commit suicide. If you suspect your saddle is broken, but aren't really sure, have it opened up and checked by a reputable dealer. Also check to make sure the stirrup bars and the billets are on securely. Since the billets attach to the girth, they help hold the saddle on the horse and must not be worn out or ready to fall off. Other accessories to check for strength and wear are girths, stirrup leathers, and stirrup irons.

Is the Stuffing Uniform?

Are the panels of your saddle stuffed evenly and smoothly? If they are stuffed irregularly or have worn-out spots, your saddle will rock. If they are overstuffed or understuffed, or are attached crookedly to the saddle, your weight will not be distributed properly and your seat will not be secure.

Is the Saddle the Right Size for Your Horse?

A saddle should distribute your weight evenly over the muscles on either side of the horse's backbone and never touch the horse's spine even when you are mounted. It should not put pressure on the horse's withers or pinch them. (A saddle that is too broad causes pressure; one that is too narrow, pinches.) It should allow the horse's shoulders and loins to move freely.

If your saddle is too large or too small, it will irritate your horse's back and hinder his performance. It will also endanger you by destroying the security of your seat and making communication impossible. Protect yourself by refusing to accept a bad fit. Modern saddles come in a wide range of sizes and styles and you can afford to be choosy.

If you feel that your horse is difficult to fit, draw a diagram of his back and bring it with you to the saddler. To draw the diagram, you will need four strips of thin, pliable wire about thirty-six inches long, four sheets of cardboard, a pencil, and a pair of scissors. Here is how to do it:

If your horse is difficult to fit for a saddle, a diagram of his back may be needed. To do this yourself, place a wire at each point indicated, bend it to the shape of the horse's body, then trace the pattern on cardboard.

1. Place one piece of wire across the horse's back, at the withers, and bend it to the shape of his body.
2. Carefully lift the wire off the horse and place it on a sheet of cardboard.
3. With the pencil, trace the shape of the wire onto the cardboard. You will now have a pattern of your horse's back at the withers. Cut it out.
4. Repeat steps 1 through 3 with the three remaining strips of wire, placing each strip four inches behind the one in front of it.

When your saddler puts the four patterns together, he will have a facsimile of your horse's entire back and will be able to fit him properly.

Is the Saddle the Right Size for You?

Make sure you try it out before you buy it. All manufacturers size differently, and you may require different sizes in different models. Also, remember that your seat can be altered by changing the length of the stirrup leathers, so be sure yours are the correct length for the type of saddle you've chosen.

Are You Buying from a Reliable Source?

A reputable dealer will allow you to return or exchange your saddle if it doesn't fit properly. Since a saddle is an important and expensive piece of equipment, and since it is usually purchased by taking the horse's measurements (see above) rather than by actual try-on, you must be allowed to correct your mistakes.

Caution: When buying a second-hand saddle, it is always safer to deal with a reputable saddler than with a "friend" at the stable. The former will check the saddle thoroughly to make sure it is sound and will stand behind the sale.

HOW TO SADDLE A HORSE SAFELY

1. Tie your horse securely so he cannot get away from you and cannot nip or kick at other horses.

2. Make sure the horse's back and girth area are clean before you saddle him. Smooth down the hair where the saddle and girth will go. No matter how clean the saddle and blanket may look, check them closely for foreign objects. A small irritant is all it takes to hurt a horse's back and start him bucking.
3. Assemble all your tack before approaching your horse, so you need not run back and forth for mislaid or forgotten items.
4. Don't let your horse be hit by dangling girths and stirrups. Attach your girth to the off-side of the saddle, then lay it back across the seat and run up the stirrups. If you have a Western saddle, lay the right cinch and stirrup across the seat.
5. Prepare to saddle your horse from the left side. While horses can and should get used to being approached, saddled, and mounted from either side, most have been trained to the left, and you will be safer if you follow suit, especially if you are dealing with an unfamiliar mount.
6. When saddling, stand behind the horse's shoulder so you are out of kicking range. Stand with your feet well back and lean forward when placing the saddle on the horse.
7. A saddle should rest just behind the horse's withers, leaving his loins and shoulders free. If you are using an English saddle, place it gently but firmly on the horse's back. It should first be placed well forward on the withers, then slid into its correct position so the hair on the horse's back remains smooth beneath it.

   Western saddles are much heavier than English ones and must be swung into position. However, make sure that you swing slowly and gently and that you don't frighten the horse by allowing the saddle to crash down on him.
8. Walk all around the horse to make sure everything under the saddle is lying flat. Then lower your girth, pass it under the horse, and buckle it just tightly enough to hold the saddle firmly in place and prevent it from slipping back. If you have a Western saddle, fasten the front

cinch first, then the rear cinch, then the strap that con-
nects the two.
9. Be sure the girth does not pinch the horse and make him
sore. Lift each of his forelegs and pull it forward to eliminate any wrinkles in his skin.
10. Check your girth adjustment three times: after you saddle your horse, after he moves a bit, after a few minutes
of riding. Since many horses purposely blow themselves
out to avoid a tight girth, you cannot get a correct fit
until they walk awhile and relax.
11. Remember that your safety depends on the quality and
condition of your equipment. Clean your tack well, and
care for it properly. (See Chapter 2.) Check it regularly for
signs of distress, and don't take chances with worn-out
straps or parts.

MOUNTING AND DISMOUNTING

It is customary to mount from the horse's left side. This tradition
is many centuries old and developed because the cavalryman
(or knight) wore his sword over his left leg and found it difficult
to swing himself into the saddle from the horse's right side.
Today, of course, there is no practical reason for favoring either
side. If you are schooling your own horse, you can and should
get him used to being approached and mounted from the left
and the right. If, however, you are riding an unfamiliar horse,
safety decrees that you follow convention and mount from the
left, since you have no way of knowing how the horse has been
trained.

When you mount and dismount, do so in a spacious area, free
of clutter. Never mount near walls, fences, trees, or overhanging branches. If your horse rears or moves suddenly, you can be
thrown against these things and hurt.

If you are riding an unfamiliar horse, spend a few minutes
making friends with him before you mount. A few minutes of
friendliness will increase your confidence in each other and lay
the groundwork for a positive relationship.

If you are mounting for the first time, don't worry about your performance and try to relax as much as possible. Most of the problems that beginners face are self-inflicted. By transmitting their nervousness to the horse, they create the kind of confusion that causes accidents.

If you are afraid of horses or are ambivalent about riding, take the time to build up your confidence. Try to overcome your fears by learning as much as you can about your prospective mount. Start by watching him in action; then get up close to him. Speak to him, pet him, offer him a treat, take him for a short walk. If personal contact does not dispel your doubts, then you had better put off mounting until you feel more secure. Communicating your anxieties to a horse can only have unpleasant results for both of you.

MOUNTING CORRECTLY

If you get a horse who won't stand still, your safety will depend on your ability to mount correctly. Mounting is an important procedure that should never be minimized or ignored. Here are three ways to do it properly. The first is the most popular.

Mounting with Stirrups

Stand near the horse's left shoulder, and face the rear, so you don't get kicked. Take the reins in your left hand to keep the horse from moving out, and rest them on the pommel of the saddle. Grasp the left stirrup iron with your right hand, turn it toward you, and put your left foot into the stirrup, being careful not to kick the horse. Transfer your right hand to the cantle of the saddle, put your weight on your left foot, and spring up off your right foot. *Note:* Always *spring* up. Never grab the saddle and attempt to *pull* yourself up.

Now, swing your right leg gently over the horse, move your right hand to the pommel, and come down lightly into the saddle. Put your right foot into the stirrup, and take up the reins.

The idea behind this method is simple: by facing the rear when you mount, you get swung into the saddle if your horse suddenly decides to take off. Were he to take off while you were facing front, you would not only lose him but be hurt in the process.

One bit of advice: when springing off that right foot to mount, try to make it up on the first jump. Repeated jumps make the horse restless and should not be necessary. A little practice will give you the needed agility.

Mounting without Stirrups

Face the saddle and put your right hand on the cantle while your left hand, with the reins, grasps the pommel. Bend your knees, push down hard with both hands, and spring up off your feet. Then, straighten your arms and let them support the weight of your body as you lift it over the saddle. Move your right hand to the pommel, swing your right leg over the horse's back, and lower yourself gently into the saddle.

Getting a Leg Up

This method requires the help of another person, but it is a safe, effortless way to mount a difficult horse.

Hold the reins in your left hand and face the saddle. Place both hands on the pommel and bend your left leg sharply at the knee. Have your assistant stand close behind you and grasp your left ankle with his right hand, while cupping your knee with his left. At a signal from you, have him lift your left leg high enough and firmly enough for you to spring off your right foot and swing your right leg over the horse's back. Then come down lightly into the saddle as usual, put your feet into the stirrups, and take up the reins.

A word of caution: It is a good idea for you and your assistant to practice this together so that in his efforts to get you into the saddle, he does not hoist you completely over the horse and onto the ground on the other side!

WHAT TO DO AFTER MOUNTING

Once you are in the saddle, there are several important steps to follow before beginning your ride:

1. Recheck the girth to make sure it is tight enough. Since a horse is apt to blow himself out (expand his stomach) when being saddled, the girth can be adjusted properly only after he has relaxed and moved a bit.
2. Be certain your stirrups are the correct length. When your legs hang straight down, the stirrup treads should be even with your ankles.
3. Check the saddle and make sure your weight has not caused it to press down on the horse's spine and withers.
4. Check the reins to make sure they are not twisted.

DISMOUNTING CORRECTLY

There are three correct ways to dismount. Whichever you choose, remember to hold onto the reins every step of the way. If you drop them, you lose control of the horse and risk serious injury.

1. Remove both feet from the stirrups, put your hands on the horse's shoulders and lean forward. Swing your right leg over the horse's croup, being careful not to touch or rub him, then jump down, and land on your toes.
2. Remove both feet from the stirrups and lean forward. With your left hand on the horse's neck and your right on the pommel, vault off, and land on your toes, taking care to avoid the horse's forelegs.

   When using this method or the first one, do not begin to dismount until you are sure both feet are free of the stirrups.
3. With your left hand holding the reins and both hands on the pommel, remove your right foot from the stirrup, lean forward, and swing your right leg back over the horse. As your leg clears his croup, transfer your right hand to the cantle for balance and let all your weight rest on your hands and arms. Remove your left foot from the stirrup, push yourself slightly away from the horse, and slide down gently.

WHAT TO DO AFTER DISMOUNTING

1. Run up the stirrups immediately. This means slide them up under the leathers and fasten them so they don't dangle. Dangling stirrups are dangerous for three reasons: they can get caught on doorways or projecting objects; their banging can startle or disturb the horse when he moves; and the horse can catch a hindfoot in one when scratching or fighting flies.
2. When you have run up the stirrups, bring the reins forward over the horse's head and use them to hold him or lead him.

EMERGENCY DISMOUNT

If ever you lose control of your horse and need to dismount quickly in order to avoid serious accident, you must use the method known as the emergency dismount.

Lean forward and put your arms around the horse's neck. Put your head to the side of his neck and remove your feet from the stirrups. Lift one leg over the horse's back, drop the reins, and swing down—on the left side, if possible. If you are riding in open country, try to find yourself a soft landing place before quitting the saddle. If you are on a road or a bridle path, aim for the safest possible place—a shrub or a bush rather than a rocky stretch of land or a tree.

Emergency dismount

TYING

Millions of years ago, the horse was a small animal surrounded by large predators. When he found he could outrun his enemies, flight—in his mind—became synonymous with survival. As long as he could run, he was safe; denied the use of his legs, he was vulnerable and helpless.

Though the modern horse no longer leads the perilous life of his ancestors and is many times larger and stronger than they were, his urge to outrun danger is as powerful as ever. Centuries of evolution have not quieted his fears. When tied up, he still feels defenseless; anxiety overwhelms him, and he does his utmost to break free.

Unfortunately, the mortality rate for runaways is high, and it is your job to see that your horse does not get loose or injure himself trying. It is also your job to calm and reassure him, so he can accept tying and remain standing in one place by himself. Though a tied horse may never be a truly happy one, most can be trained to stand well if their needs are met and proper precautions are taken.

WHERE TO TIE YOUR HORSE

Choose a spot you yourself consider comfortable. If the weather is warm, keep your horse in the shade and apply insect repellent to discourage flies. Never tie him near branches or shrubbery that can entangle him, near horses who can fight with him, or near noisy farm or garden equipment that can frighten him. Since he loves to play with insignificant but dangerous pieces of rubbish, avoid areas that contain broken glass and other bits of debris.

Never tie your horse to a wheeled object that will roll around and frighten him or to a barbed wire fence that will cut him up. Remember that he is very strong and must be tied to something solid and immovable, not something that will break or come loose. Trees, fence posts (not fences), posts set in concrete, and hitch rails are all safe. Rails and boards are not.

WHAT TO TIE HIM WITH

A horse is usually tied with a lead rope that is knotted directly to the ring of his halter. However, in deciding what kind of halter and lead to use, we are faced with something of a dilemma. Although we want strong equipment that will keep the horse in check, we must recognize the fact that, when a truly frantic horse fights unbreakable ties, he is likely to strangle on them, and he would stand a better chance of survival by breaking loose and running away. Therefore, use equipment that will not break easily, that will take plenty of stress, but *will* give way under *unusual pressure*, for instance, cotton or leather halters and leather or sisal lead ropes. A sharp pocketknife is also a necessity for anyone who works around horses. Be sure you always carry one with you in case you have to cut a tangled horse loose in a hurry.

Caution: Never tie a horse by his bridle or by his bridle reins. Both will snap. If, for some reason, you have to leave the bridle on, slip a halter over it and fasten the tie rope to that. To keep the horse from snaring himself in the reins, place them under the stirrups of an English saddle or tie them around the horn of a Western saddle.

THE CORRECT KNOT

A quick-release knot is the only knot used to tie a horse. Although strong enough to resist the pulling of a frightened ani-

Quick release knot

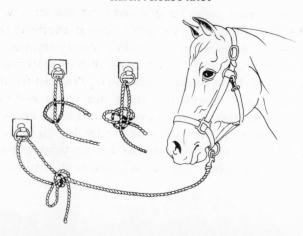

mal, it opens immediately to the tug of a human hand. As you can see from the diagram, it is easy to learn and, once mastered, allows you to tie your horse correctly every time.

Slipknots, which tighten quickly around the object they enclose, must never be used anywhere on a horse's body.

TYING CORRECTLY

A horse can be tied anywhere above his withers. If he fights his ties, he will hurt himself less on a high rope than on a low one, which is apt to injure his neck.

Give your horse just enough rope to allow him to touch the ground with his nose. Give him more, and he will tangle himself up in it. Give him less, and he will grow restless over his cramped condition. Either way, the result will be panic, pulling, and, possibly, a bad rope burn.

If you tie your horse in a straight stall, give him just enough rope to allow him to lie down comfortably.

If you use a lariat or a lunge line for tying, be careful not to trip over the coils.

HOW TO BEHAVE AROUND A TIED HORSE

Remember that your horse has a strong herd instinct. He does not like to be alone, and it is not wise to leave him untended for long periods of time. If he is going to be standing by himself for a while, see that you provide some water and hay to occupy him and give him a feeling of well-being, and come back regularly to check on him.

Never take a tied horse for granted—no matter how well he accepts his ties, he will try to break loose if anything frightens him. Approach him only in a calm, steady manner. Avoid sudden movements and loud noises. When walking around him, stay beyond the reach of his heels. Walk in front of him only if you know him well and know him to be well behaved. Even then, walk carefully and speak to him so he knows where you are. Never step over or walk under his tie rope. When working around him, make sure he knows your exact whereabouts. Never remove his halter without first untying him.

IF YOU CANNOT TRAIN YOUR HORSE TO STAND TIED

There are some horses who never seem to get over their fear of being tied. These are called halter-pullers because they pull and jump until they either break loose or wear themselves out in the attempt.

If you have a halter-puller, it is important to get help from a professional horseman or trainer. Your return in safety and satisfaction will outweigh any cost involved.

BANDAGING

Bandages are applied to a horse's legs and tail to prevent injury when he is working or traveling and also to treat injury. However, they are effective only if they are used intelligently and wrapped properly. Incorrect usage and faulty application will do more to harm the horse than to help him.

Use bandages only when absolutely necessary. A horse needs to be bandaged when he is under stress, when he is working *hard,* when he has a specific problem, or when he is traveling. He does not need to be bandaged for everyday riding or for light work. Many riders mistakenly use bandages for all workouts, believing that they will spare the horse's legs. However, the object of working out is to strengthen and build up those legs. If

How to bandage the legs of a horse

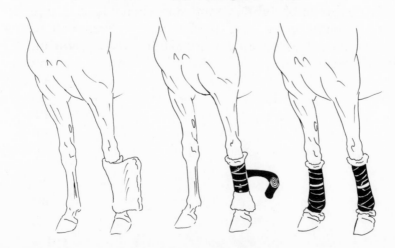

they are always in bandages, the muscles and tendons will weaken, and the horse will be more—not less—likely to sustain an injury.

Follow these rules whenever you apply leg bandages:

1. Use several layers of cotton padding under each bandage. Padding helps to distribute pressure evenly and prevents pressure sores.
2. Start the bandage just below the knee and end it just below the coronary band if it is to be used for shipping. If it is to be used only for support, end it at the fetlock.
3. Wind the bandage clockwise so that if the horse hits it with his other leg, it will loosen, not tighten.
4. Allow some cotton padding to stick out at the top and bottom of the bandage, so the horse can flex his leg without being chafed.
5. Tape down the ends of the bandage to keep them from untying.

When you apply a leg or tail bandage to prevent injury, never wrap it too tightly or leave it on more than twenty-four hours. Either mistake may bow a tendon or result in a loss of tail hair. In extreme cases, when the bandage is left on for several days or is unusually tight, the horse may lose his entire tail—too much pressure can cause the tail artery to collapse—or an entire foot.

To make sure you are applying your bandages properly, wrap one around your own arm or leg. If the limb falls asleep from lack of circulation, you are wrapping too tightly. The only time a bandage should be tightly wrapped is when it is used to reduce swelling or to stop bleeding (see Chapter 11). Even then, it must be rewound at least once a day to make sure it is not affecting the horse's circulation.

RIDING SAFELY

If you are riding for the first time, you can't help but wonder: Will my horse bolt? Will he throw me? Will I get hurt?

You may be surprised to learn that the way your horse behaves and the type of ride you get depend largely on you.

A horse will seldom hurt you intentionally. His nature is normally gentle and friendly, and he tries hard to perform what is expected of him. However, he has many fears, and in order to do his job well he must resist the impulse to bolt and strike out whenever he is frightened.

You alone can help him. If you provide the right kind of guidance, he will develop enough confidence to overcome his anxiety and behave responsibly. If you don't, or if you can't, he will panic easily and become a menace to himself and others around him.

Your safety depends on your performance and your technique. The more technically expert you become, the safer you will be. Riding is not a haphazard sport, and no rider is at the mercy of mysterious, unknown forces. The rules of the game are clearly spelled out, and the disciplines can be mastered by anyone willing to make the effort. Those that do will find they can handle almost any situation that arises and make their riding the safe, satisfying experience it was meant to be.

RIDING BASICS

A rider conveys instructions to a horse through his seat, hands, legs, voice, and body. These are called the *natural aids,* and they are applied both separately and in combination.

THE SEAT AND THE BODY

The rider and the horse move as one body and, consequently, have the same center of gravity. If the rider shifts his weight in the saddle, the horse must make a corresponding shift in order to maintain his balance. This principle helps the rider to change the horse's direction by changing his own position.

THE HANDS

The reins give the rider a direct line to the horse's mouth and enable him to regulate the horse's movements and his balance. Steady hands will keep a horse moving straight ahead. Hands that move continuously will confuse the horse and obscure the rider's message.

THE LEGS

The legs help the hands to direct and control the horse. They rule the hindquarters and create impulsion by applying pressure to the horse's sides.

THE VOICE

Voice timbre can sometimes influence behavior: a calm, gentle voice may quiet and reassure a frightened horse; stern warnings may check a disobedient one. While horses can be taught to associate words with deeds, voice signals are not used extensively in training.

Natural aids are sometimes augmented by *artificial aids*, such as whips, spurs, and martingales. Martingales keep the horse from carrying his head above the angle of control, while whips and spurs reinforce the leg aids whenever necessary. Spurs are tricky and should be worn only by advanced riders who can devote special attention to their type, use, and fit.

The aids make it possible for you to control your horse—to tell him what to do and when to do it. This control is crucial to your safety. Although you must never nag or pester your horse, you must nonetheless maintain the upper hand at all times and suppress any contrariness at its inception. A rider who allows a horse to ignore instructions and do as he pleases is asking for trouble.

PERFECTING YOUR TECHNIQUE

A rider's first task is to acquire a good, firm position in the saddle, one that will remain intact no matter how the horse misbehaves.

Begin by sitting upright on your horse, with your thighs on the saddle and your knees well rolled in. Keep your lower legs straight and your heels slightly turned down. To improve your balance, focus your eyes between the horse's ears so you can follow the direction he is moving in. Try not to bend forward or shorten your reins whenever you feel insecure. Instead, keep your shoulders back and remain in position. You will find that if you sit correctly, it is far more difficult to fall off the horse than to stay on.

Always remember that you communicate instructions to your horse through your seat, therefore you must avoid any movement that is not meant to convey a message. The horse's back is very sensitive, and he will interpret the slightest shift of emphasis as a command. If you constantly move around in the saddle, you will send contradictory signals that confuse and rattle him.

Work hard to perfect your balance and strengthen your grip. When you can maintain a strong, steady position in the saddle without depending on reins or stirrups for support, you will have achieved the ultimate: an independent seat. This is the best safety insurance you can have, and it should be acquired early in your riding career. The following exercises will help you get it, but be sure to do them on a quiet horse and have a friend control the horse's head.

EXERCISES FOR BALANCE

1. Release the reins and grasp the pommel. Keeping your legs still, turn your body first to the left, then to the right. Lean as far forward and as far back as you can. Stand up in the saddle, then slowly sit down again.
2. When you have mastered the above exercises, fold your arms and try to do them without holding on to the pommel.
3. Extend your arms to the sides. Moving both arms together and in the same direction, make small circles, then larger ones.
4. With your arms extended to the sides, twist your body first to the left, then to the right. Twist your trunk only.
5. Relax your arms. Remove your feet from the stirrups and swing your legs backward and forward, from the knees down. As one leg goes forward, the other should go back, and vice versa.
6. Rotate your feet from the ankles down. Rotate both feet at the same time and in the same direction.

As with all exercises, repetition increases proficiency. The more you do, the more balance (and confidence) you acquire. When, at last, you feel so relaxed and secure in the saddle that you and your horse move as one body, you will have achieved your goal.

Exercises for balance

RIDING PROBLEMS

Horses, like people, are subject to strong emotions and often express them in frightening ways. Faced with fear, anger, or frustration, they may kick, rear, bolt, or do any number of things potentially dangerous to themselves and others.

Fortunately, there are effective ways of dealing with such behavior. A trained rider with a calm approach and an independent seat can usually bring a wayward horse under control without harming himself or his mount. Often, he can thwart the waywardness by recognizing its symptoms in advance and taking quick, preventive action. Knowing what to do and when to do it is always a rider's best defense against injury and panic.

TRIPPING

When a horse trips, it is generally because he is tired or poorly ridden. To help him regain his balance, keep his head erect and apply leg pressure. This will gather his hindquarters under him and decrease the weight on his forelegs so he can right himself more easily.

Keeping your horse alert at all times, particularly when going downhill, will usually prevent tripping. However, any horse who trips repeatedly should be checked for navicular disease (inflammation of the navicular bone).

STOPPING

A startled or frightened horse will either shy or stop abruptly and refuse to move. If your horse stops, don't punish him or try to force him forward. Wait and see if he goes of his own accord. If he doesn't, try turning him to the left or right. Forcing him to shift his balance should start him up again. If it doesn't, dismount and lead him forward or else put a more confident horse in front of him.

KICKING AND BUCKING

If your horse drops his bit for a moment or two, it usually means he is about to misbehave. If he lays his ears straight back, it means he is angry, irritated, or about to kick. The trick here is to take quick action: apply leg pressure and keep the horse moving, so he is unable to get his hind legs into kicking position or use them for any mischief. If he drops his head, bring it back up with a few tugs on the reins and keep your balance by sitting normally. To thwart a bucking horse, keep his head turned and walk him around in circles.

If you have a chronic kicker, don't let him get close to other horses, and tie a red ribbon on his tail as a warning to other riders.

REARING

If your horse rears, remember that he will continue to do so unless you can get him back on the bit. Do this by repeatedly pressing your legs against his sides and by keeping a light, steady feeling on the reins.

If this doesn't work, force the horse down by turning his head. Hold the reins in both hands, slacken one, and pull just enough on the other to move his head to one side. Once his head turns, he can only maintain his balance by dropping down on all fours. When he does, walk him around in tight circles until he relaxes.

Unfortunately, the effectiveness of these maneuvers is offset by their difficulty. Both are way beyond the average rider's ability and demand the nerve and skill of an expert. Non-pros will find them highly dangerous.

If your horse continues to rear, you can use a tight standing martingale to keep him from raising his head above the level of control, but this is only a partial solution. Your best bet is to sell him.

RUNNING AWAY

Although a horse may bolt out of nervousness or fear, the most common catalyst is pain—pain from heavy hands, from an aching mouth, or from improper equipment. Before you panic, remember that a runaway horse will not go any faster than a normal one at a fast gallop—and a good rider should have no trouble keeping his seat. In most cases, he will even be able to feel when the horse is about to bolt and check him before he gets a chance to do so.

In the event that you fail to stop your horse from bolting, drive your seat into the saddle, keep one hand still, and pull on the reins with the other. Never lean back in the saddle and pull on both reins at the same time. To steady yourself, grip the saddle with your knees but be sure to keep your lower legs away from the horse, since even a slight brush of your heels will spur him on. Calm him down by speaking to him as quietly as possible and, if the area permits, by walking him around in tight circles.

Given sufficient space, a confident rider will often allow a bolting horse to keep on running, feeling that once the initial thrust is over, the horse can be easily subdued. Also, a horse who is given such unexpected freedom will frequently stop out of sheer surprise.

IF YOU FALL

Learning how to fall should be a compulsory part of every rider's training. Though falls occur suddenly, there are still several things you can do to minimize your injuries and spare yourself undue pain.

Always ride with a safety hat. Make sure you wear boots with heels and avoid stirrups that are too large or too small for you. If one of your feet slips through a stirrup or gets wedged inside it when you fall, you will not be able to free it and you will be dragged along the ground.

If you feel you are falling, let yourself go as limp as possible. Although your natural impulse will be to tighten up, try relaxing instead. The more relaxed you are, the less you will be jarred when your body hits the ground.

If it seems to you that, on falling, you would hit a dangerous object, try to propel yourself beyond it by pushing against your horse as you are thrust from the saddle.

Hold on to the reins only until you are clear of the horse. If you continue to hold on to them after you have fallen, you may pull the horse over on top of you.

When falling, make your body as compact as you can and

keep your arms and legs well tucked in. If you stick an arm out to break your fall, you may break the arm instead.

When your body hits the ground, roll as far away from your horse as you possibly can. This will get you out of his path if he falls or runs away.

HOW TO RIDE SAFELY

Do not hurry your early training. Bad habits are quickly acquired, good ones develop slowly. A strong foundation requires time and effort but ultimately enriches all your riding experiences.

Never ask for more horse than you can handle. While most people ride for exercise or pleasure, some ride for pure excitement and are seldom satisfied with a competent mount. These individuals are always after more horse, more action, and usually wind up with more trouble than they can cope with.

If your horse is bursting with energy, or if he has not been ridden for several days, lunge him with his saddle on for a few moments before you mount. This will give him time to relax and literally "get his back down"—when his back first feels the weight of the saddle, his muscles tighten and tense up, and he is apt to kick or rear. Turning him loose for a while will make him safer to ride.

Always give your horse a good warm-up before you put him to work. Begin your ride with a ten-minute walk and trot, so you don't strain his muscles or damage his wind.

Ride in an enclosed area or an arena until you know your horse and are familiar with his habits.

Master the walk and the trot in school and on the road before you try to canter or gallop. Accidents occur more frequently at the faster paces because the horse and rider are more likely to lose their balance when speeding. Put your horse into top gear only if you are equipped to control him.

Learn to keep your horse in hand at all times so he can carry out your instructions immediately on command. A horse who is not in hand is incapable of carrying out an order.

Make sure you really ride your horse at all times—never leave him to his own devices or let down your guard. Firm handling increases a horse's confidence in his rider, and the more he trusts, the less he acts up.

Always keep your horse moving straight ahead, and keep up his pace. A horse who meanders from side to side is a menace to others on the road, and one who shuffles along can trip and break his knees.

Horses must be kept alert and on the bit at all times, and must maintain an even gait. Many pick up speed when headed for home, and this is one distressing habit that should be quickly checked. Grazing during a ride is another. If your horse bends his head, bring it back up with a kick and a good, hard pull. Even if he doesn't ingest any sprayed grass, he can swell up from overeating and cause his girth to tighten and pinch. Horses should also be kept away from ponds and streams, particularly in warm weather when water is so attractive.

RIDING ON THE PUBLIC ROAD

Today's thoroughfares must accommodate pedestrians, cars, trucks, trailers, cycles, and countless other moving vehicles. To ensure everyone's safety, observe the rules of the road and respect the rights of those using it.

Ride on the side of the road designated for you by law. This will vary from state to state, so check local regulations for details. Ride on the bridle path or on the shoulder of the road. Try to avoid paved roads or roads with hard surfaces. Do not ride over lawns or farmland. Do not ride on footpaths. These are for the use of pedestrians and should not be mussed up by horses. Do not ride over other people's property, unless you have permission to do so. When visiting friends, never tie your horse near any object he can trample or destroy.

Stay alert at all times. Look left and right before starting out, turning, or stopping. Be prepared for unexpected movements by pedestrians, cars, and all other roadway vehicles. Look ahead of you, behind you, and to the side for developing trouble spots. Slow down at all intersections. Look left and right before crossing. If the road is clear, walk across quickly. If it isn't, wait patiently, without fussing. In heavy traffic areas, follow the safest course: dismount and lead your horse.

Remember that you are required by law to obey all traffic

rules and regulations. This means you must learn the meanings of all lights, signs, and signals.

Traffic Lights

Most traffic lights have two or three colors.

three-color light   two-color light

Green means proceed.
Red means stop, wait for the green light before proceeding.
Yellow warns that a red light is about to appear.
On two-color lights, a combined red and green signal or a dark period have the same meaning as the yellow warning light.

A green arrow means that you have permission to move in the direction indicated by the arrow.

A flashing red light is the equivalent of a stop sign. It means you must come to a complete halt before entering the intersection in question.

A flashing yellow light means proceed with caution.

Traffic lights may be disregarded *only when a traffic officer on duty* gives you alternate directions. In such instances, these directions take precedence over all other signals.

Traffic Signs

The following are eighteen common road signs. Some give specific directions; others are warnings. *All* are important, so be sure you know their meanings.

Come to a full stop when you reach the intersection. Yield the right-of-way to any vehicle that enters the intersection from another road, then proceed with caution.

Slow down as you approach the intersection. If the intersection is clear, proceed without stopping. If pedestrians or other vehicles are passing, stop and yield them the right-of-way.

RAILROAD CROSSING

NO U-TURN

ONE WAY TRAFFIC
DO NOT ENTER

NO LEFT TURN

SCHOOL

SCHOOL CROSSING

NO
TURN
ON
RED

NO RIGHT TURN

DIVIDED
HIGHWAY ENDS

TRAFFIC SIGNAL
AHEAD

TWO-WAY
TRAFFIC

MERGING TRAFFIC
ENTERING FROM
RIGHT

HILL AHEAD

SCHOOL CROSSING

SLIPPERY WHEN WET

HOSPITAL
EMERGENCY
SERVICES—
TO THE RIGHT

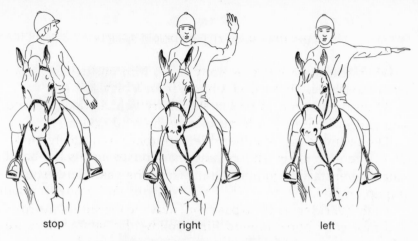

stop   right   left

Directional signals on horseback

Hand Signals

Always give the appropriate signal when slowing down, stopping, or making a turn. When riding *with* the traffic, signal with your left hand; when riding *against* the traffic, signal with your right. When making a left turn, put your arm straight out. When making a right turn, point your arm up. When slowing down or stopping, point your arm down.

Always give your signal clearly and give it at least one hundred feet before you make your turn or stop.

Right-of-Way

You must always yield the right-of-way to: ambulances, fire engines, and other emergency vehicles; pedestrians at crosswalks; any vehicle going straight ahead, if you plan to turn left; any vehicle on a main road, if you enter the road from a driveway or side street; any vehicle already in an intersection, if you have not yet entered it.

Always ride with extreme caution in high-risk areas such as parks, playgrounds, bus stops, and school zones.

If you see a school bus loading or unloading, approach it carefully—children may run across your path without warning. All school buses are painted bright yellow and bear the words *School Bus* in large black letters on the back and front of the bus. Back and front are also equipped with red lights that flash whenever the door opens to admit or discharge passengers. *Never pass the bus until the light goes off.*

When leading a horse or pony, keep him on the side *away* from the traffic. Never lead a horse from a bicycle.

When pulling out to pass a stationary vehicle, look behind you and in front of you to make sure the road is clear.

If you want to pass another rider, approach him slowly, make your intention clear, and advance cautiously on his left-hand side. Never startle another horse by running past him or sneaking up on him.

If another rider wants to pass you, move to the side of the road and face your horse toward him. Follow the same procedure whenever any vehicle passes you on a narrow road.

Always be courteous and help others on the road. Acknowledge their courtesy to you with a friendly "Thank You." A driver who is forced to slow down or stop for you will be more inclined to oblige the next rider if he knows his actions are genuinely appreciated.

Cautionary Notes

When riding on the public road, keep your horse at a walk. Walk especially when passing others on the bridle path, when approaching and going over bridges, and when going through underpasses. Walk whenever mud, sand, ice, or snow put you in danger of slipping or falling.

You may trot for short distances, provided you trot slowly. Fast trotting on a hard surface causes concussion in the horse's feet and lower limbs, and can lead to lameness.

Always be on the lookout for a sudden change in footing. When riding on rough ground or going down steep hills or rocky terrain, go slowly, or else dismount and lead your horse.

When climbing hills, adjust your pace to the terrain. Trotting uphill for a short time is good strengthening exercise but should be done slowly on hard-surfaced roads.

When climbing a steep hill with *uncertain* terrain, walk your horse, or else dismount and lead him up it. However, if the going is good, you can canter—your horse can't possibly run away with you and he'll be more than happy to stop when he reaches the top.

The important thing to remember when going up or down hill

is to keep your weight off the horse's hindquarters. When going uphill, lean forward and hold on to the mane or the pommel. When going downhill, incline your body forward ever so slightly. Although the natural tendency in both cases is to lean back in the saddle, such action will restrict your horse's movement and make it difficult for him to keep his balance.

On a long ride, be considerate of your horse and give him an opportunity to rest and refresh himself. Stop, dismount, and loosen his girth. An easy walk, followed by a few quiet moments alone, will cool him down.

Always walk the last mile home. A horse who is taken back to the stable hot is likely to catch a chill.

Speak to your insurance agent about personal liability insurance. Every horse owner should have a policy that covers him for damages incurred by his horse.

Riding in Traffic

The majority of horses learn to take traffic in their stride and remain largely undisturbed by it. However, even the most reliable horse will occasionally develop an aversion to some object and shy away from it. The offender may be something foreign to the horse's experience, like an airplane, something noisy, like farm machinery, or even something completely innocent, like a rock or twig lying across a path. Weather conditions, particularly, create many effects that horses find disturbing: wind sets leaves spinning, awnings flapping, and debris flying; rain brings umbrellas and puddles—a car splashing through a puddle can suddenly terrify a horse normally oblivious of cars. The problem, then, is how to offset the horse's natural skittishness so you and he can ride safely through traffic. The following suggestions should help:

● If you see something you think will frighten your horse, or if you actually feel the beginnings of a shy, try to keep your horse moving forward. Grip your reins firmly, drive your seat into the saddle, and apply leg pressure. Hopefully, these sudden movements will divert his attention from the distressing object and cause him to go right by it. However, if you see that he is really frightened, you had better dismount and walk him past it.

- If your horse shies at oncoming cars, never turn his head away from one to keep him from seeing it. He has excellent sideway vision and he will see it anyway. Moreover, by turning his head *away* from the car, you will make his hindquarters swing out toward the road. Then, if he shies, he will end up in the middle of traffic. On the other hand, if you incline his head *toward* the approaching car and kick him with your left leg, he will be compelled to move to the right—away from the traffic and off to the side of the road.
- Shying can be highly contagious when riding in company. One shyer in a group can make even the quietest horse misbehave. To prevent chain reactions, try to station the most trustworthy horse up front when a car approaches, in the rear when a car comes from behind. If this horse remains calm, chances are the others will also.
- If a speeding car threatens to disturb the horses in your group, motion the driver to slow down. Most will oblige.
- If your horse shies frequently, try to determine the reason why. If a traumatic experience in the past has left him nervous and edgy, a firm hand and a sympathetic attitude will eventually restore his nerve. However, if he is merely being temperamental, he will need some strong words and a slap on the side to change his attitude.

RIDING IN COMPANY

Be courteous at all times and do nothing to trouble another rider.

Wait until all the riders in your group are mounted before you ride off. Horses are herd animals and if one moves out, the others may follow.

Never ride too close to the back of another horse. If you are not riding abreast, keep a full horse's length behind the horse in front of you. Be sure each rider in your group has sufficient space to navigate.

The leader of the group should keep to a steady pace so the

rear file need never rush to catch up. Before crossing a road, he should make sure it is clear enough for the whole party to cross in safety, and then make sure all the riders are close enough to cross together. Separations—with some riders on one side of the road and some on the other—should be avoided.

The last rider to pass through a gate is responsible for closing it. However, others in his party should not ride off without him since his efforts to catch up can create a disturbance.

When riding in company, don't get so involved in conversation that you become oblivious of conditions on the road. Above all, never fool around on horseback. "Horseplay" is always out of place around horses.

When riding in a group, never issue verbal commands to your horse. Other horses in the party may obey them as well.

If one of your party stops his horse during a ride, make sure you follow suit. If you don't, the other horse may keep on going and upset his rider.

Stopping is also advisable when another rider's horse bolts. If you pursue the runaway, he will only quicken his pace. Stopping may slow him down or bring him to a halt. Should you find yourself ahead of the delinquent on the bridle path, wait until he approaches you, then fall in alongside him and grab his reins. If you miss, let him go on alone. Again, don't bother to run after him. Have the rest of your group return home and, chances are, the prodigal will follow.

If you are thrown, always try to hang on to the reins *until you are clear of the horse*—they will enable you to slow him down a bit if your foot catches in the stirrup. (See "If You Fall," Chapter 4.) If, when you hit the ground, you are in the path of some oncoming danger, get up immediately and move to safety. However, if you are in no danger, stay where you are and wait quietly for your companions to ride over. When they do, your sociable horse will probably wander over to be near his fellows. Should he stop nearby, get to your feet slowly. Jumping up quickly may startle him into running off again.

OPENING AND CLOSING GATES

Since fence and garden gates must be securely fastened at all times, learn to open and close them properly from the back of a horse. The butt end of a moderate-size whip or crop will help you manipulate the hooks and latches.

If a gate opens toward you, ride up close to it, unlatch it, and hold it open until your horse walks through it. The horse should then stand parallel to the opening so that you face the catch and can lean over and pull the gate closed with your whip.

If a gate opens away from you, stand parallel to it, with your face toward the catch and your back toward the hinges. Undo the catch with your whip butt and push open the gate. To close it, stand beside it and push it shut.

Remember the following

- Some horses are upset by the sight of a whip. Keep yours as inconspicuous as possible. Also, be sure you choose one of moderate length. A long one will make you clumsy and heavy-handed.

Opening a gate on horseback

- When passing through a gateway, never allow the gate to swing out and hit the horse.
- When closing a gate, never ride away until you make sure the catch has engaged. If it remains open, other animals may pass through and either cause damage or go astray.
- Never let your horse help you open gates and unfasten latches. Once he becomes adept at it—and he will—he will use his talents on the stable door.

RIDING AT NIGHT

Riding at night can be a pleasure or a pain, depending on your romantic inclinations, your spirit of adventure, and your ability to manage a horse. While limited visibility is unquestionably a hazard, special safety measures can minimize, if not eliminate, the danger.

If possible, ride on a moonlit night so you have some source of light. Carry a flashlight at all times. When riding indoors, select an arena with floodlights.

When riding outdoors, choose your itinerary with special care. Ride on a familiar bridle path in an area you know to be safe, open, and devoid of debris.

Though your horse will quickly get used to being out at night and is a better nighttime navigator than most human beings, keep him at a walk. Any faster pace invites trouble.

Make absolutely certain that your horse can be seen in the dark by others on the road. Tie a white handkerchief to his tail or attach a red reflector to the outside of his left stirrup iron. Check your local saddle shop to see if new safety devices have come on the market. Also, remember that light-colored horses can be seen more easily than dark ones. If you are riding in a group, the palest horse should bring up the rear. You yourself should wear light-colored clothing.

RIDING IN WINTER

With the proper protection and very little extra effort, you and your horse can enjoy riding in winter and, at the same time, get yourselves in fine physical shape for spring. If you begin hibernating when the thermometer falls, you not only miss an exhilarating experience but deprive your horse—and yourself—of healthy, beneficial exercise. Contrary to what you might expect, horses are well equipped by nature to withstand cold and, if they are properly cared for and fed, their bodies remain warm even in sub-zero temperatures. Although they should be blanketed in twenty-degree weather (or below), the only shelter they really need is a simple lean-to to keep out icy winds. Heating is unnecessary and can even be harmful, since overly stuffy stalls invite coughs and respiratory infections.

Do Horses Need Special Equipment for Winter Riding?

Horses need special footwear to give them traction on slippery surfaces and to prevent ice and frozen earth from cracking and chipping their feet. On hard surfaces, they should wear borium-calked shoes (screw-in calks are also available) or "Easyboots" with borium studs. The latter can be put on or taken off easily to comply with the terrain.

In soft snow, boots are not worn, and snowballs are likely to form inside the hooves. Since "snowballing" can be dangerous to horse and rider alike, you must stop frequently during your ride and pick out your horse's feet, or else see that they are protected with convex hoof pads. Heavy grease will also keep out snow, but it wears off quickly and must be constantly reapplied.

Although a horse can wear a metal bit in winter, the bit should be held in the rider's hands for a few minutes before being inserted into the horse's mouth. Unless it is properly warmed up, the horse's tongue will stick to the freezing metal.

A horse never needs to be blanketed for a winter ride. In fact, if he is covered in any way when working out, he will begin to sweat and can become seriously ill.

How Much Work Should a Horse Do in Winter?

Winter work should always be moderate. It should never make the horse perspire or bring him to the point where he must take great gulps of air in order to breathe. Frozen air inhaled in this manner can hurt the sensitive membranes of his nasal passage.

Also, never ask a horse to jump in snow. He will easily lose his footing on the uncertain terrain.

Do Horses Need Special Care in Winter?

Surprisingly, it is easier to keep a horse clean in winter than in warm weather. Dried sweat is no longer a problem, and even though coats are heavier, they can be brought up to spring and summer standards with the right grooming. Legs, however, require extra attention to prevent chapped or cracked heels and pasterns. These areas must be dried thoroughly and lubricated with zinc oxide or petroleum jelly. Ice is no problem since it melts away by itself, but caked-on mud will need to be removed with a warm rinse. You will also need to beware of salt, which is sometimes sprinkled over walks, rings, tracks, and arenas to keep the ground from freezing. In addition to cracking and dehydrating the horse's skin, it can produce weeping wounds in the pastern area.

When your ride is over, use a linament rub to restore the horse's circulation. Then dress him in a wool or mesh cooler, to bring his body temperature back to normal.

How Should a Rider Dress for Winter?

Begin by forgetting about "correct" riding attire, and choose your clothes for warmth and flexibility. Since different temperatures call for different types of clothing, use the following as a guide:

FOR TEMPERATURES BETWEEN 20 AND 32 DEGREES:

Regular riding clothes can still be worn, but add thermal underwear, ski socks, lined gloves, and a warm hat. A light, lined nylon ski jacket will keep out the wind.

FOR TEMPERATURES BETWEEN 10 AND 20 DEGREES:

Wear a goosedown jacket or fleece-lined parka, a ski mask, and a scarf to keep the back of your neck warm. Goosedown jackets and vests are particularly good for cold weather riding, because they are lightweight and provide great warmth.

Make sure your gloves are fur lined or foam insulated.

Wear leather rather than rubber boots. (Leather breathes; rubber traps and condenses air.) To keep out ice and snow, cover the boots with larger overshoes.

Never wear snowmobile boots. Although many garments worn by snowmobilers are ideal for cold-weather riding, the boots have a gripping sole that makes them difficult to withdraw from stirrups.

FROM BELOW ZERO TO 10 DEGREES

The insulated overalls worn by snowmobilers are perfect for riding in freezing temperatures. Get them large enough to allow you free and easy movement, even with layers of undergarments. Also, get your boots large enough to accommodate several pairs of heavy socks.

TRAIL RIDING

HOW TO PREPARE FOR A TRAIL RIDE

Make sure your horse has the right temperament for a trail ride. A good trail horse should be relaxed and able to move out freely. He should be able to maintain an easy pace and remain alert to his surroundings at all times. He must respond well to reining, checking, and backing signals. If he overreacts to your touch or to his environment, if he is nervous or bad-tempered, he will not be a safe trail horse. Horses whose tails twitch continuously, whose ears are always pinned down, and whose eyes narrow when you touch them are also unreliable and generally irritable and sour by nature.

If you have any reason to doubt your horse's suitability for the trail, replace him immediately or postpone your trip. Trail conditions constantly test the abilities of a horse and rider, and you must have a trustworthy mount. A horse whose disposition is questionable under normal circumstances will certainly be a danger under difficult ones.

Ask your vet what shots your horse must have for the ride and make sure he gets them all. If your horse has not been properly inoculated and spreads disease to another horse, you can be held legally responsible. You yourself should have a tetanus shot.

If someone other than yourself is providing feed for the ride, find out what kind it is so you can get your horse used to it *before* you leave. Trail riding places a horse under stress, and a change of rations at such a time can cause colic and other problems.

Give your horse's hooves a thorough going-over with the hoof pick to make sure they are free of impediments.

Check all your equipment for cracks, tears, and breaks. Trail rides can be very hard on tack, and it is a good idea to replace all worn-out straps and leathers and all rusted metal and broken hardware *before* you leave home. That way you reduce the possibility of accident and eliminate time-consuming repairs en route. It is also advisable to clean your equipment at least a day before you leave so that it has a chance to dry out completely before being used.

Get as much information as possible about the area you plan to ride in. Get accurate, up-to-date maps, and check out the climate and terrain. If you are riding on state or federal lands, contact park or forest officials for regulations governing use of the trails.

Try never to ride out alone, but if you do, leave your itinerary with a friend and tell him when you plan to return.

WHAT TO TAKE ALONG

On any trail ride, you may find yourself in an emergency situation where outside help is not readily available. Make yourself as self-sufficient as possible by carrying the following equipment:

- Comfortable, protective clothing—jeans, breeches, or jodhpurs that fit well and will not rub you
- Raincoat or slicker
- First-aid kit containing gauze, tape, antiseptic, gall salve, pressure bandage, powder to stop bleeding
- A hoof pick—probably the most important piece of equipment you can have with you on the trail

- A good pocketknife and a wire cutter—to free you or your horse from entangling ropes, wires, etc.
- An extra halter and lead rope
- At least two layers of clean blanketing
- A length of rope
- A flashlight with new alkaline batteries
- Fly repellent—for you and your horse
- Matches
- Pieces of leather for repairs

SAFETY ON THE TRAIL

Consider your horse's welfare and his feelings at all times. Avoid overtiring him. In hot weather, cool him down before you water him. Watch him carefully for any injury or change of mood. Watch the position of his ears. If they move back, he is probably about to kick and should be stopped. If he seems to be disturbed, try to determine the cause. A horse will sometimes behave strangely when passing from a bright area into a dark one, and vice versa, because his eyes adjust slowly to changes in light.

As you follow a trail, take a good look at the surrounding countryside and remember landmarks for future reference.

Always expect the unexpected. Cars, motorcycles, children, birds, and animals are apt to pop out at you from the most unlikely places, creating all kinds of noise and commotion. Try to stay calm and reward your horse for good behavior when the disturbance has passed.

Do not speed. Maintain a safe pace and be careful where you ride. When you come to a boggy or muddy place, dismount and test the ground with a stick or your foot, to make sure it is strong enough to support you and your horse.

Stay away from sharp rocks. If they are unavoidable, lead your horse over or around them. Also lead him around high logs, fallen branches, and chopped-off roots that cannot be easily jumped or maneuvered.

Take nothing for granted. The most innocent-looking terrain can be tricky. Uneven mounds of soft dirt often conceal holes. So do grassy meadows. If you can't avoid these areas, take them slowly.

Having to cross a river, stream, or bridge can upset a horse. However, a slow approach, coupled with a permissive attitude, should reassure him until he gets his courage up. Urge him on gently, and reward every positive step, but also allow him to stop or drink whenever he wants. Never force the issue, but never allow him to jump over the obstacle. Your object is to make him cross it calmly, by reducing his fears and increasing his confidence.

Steep embankments are always hazardous. To attack them properly, you must consider their size and type, and the quality of footing they offer.

A straight bank can be jumped provided it is no more than half the horse's height. Heights greater than three feet should be negotiated only by an experienced trail horse. Graded, or sloping, banks need to be climbed or, if the terrain permits, slid down. When scaling a bank, lean forward and hold on to the mane or pommel so your weight does not interfere with the horse's hindquarters. When coming down, lean slightly forward for the same reason.

When resting or camping, tie your horse in a safe place and tie him securely. The correct way to tie a horse is outlined in Chapter 3 and should be read by anyone planning a trail ride.

Keep your gear neat and accessible. Secure it well so it does not flop around and annoy the horse or become entangled and cause an accident.

Remember that forest fires destroy life and property and waste our natural resources. Never be careless with matches, cigarettes, or campfires. Make sure all are completely snuffed out before you leave them.

TRAIL RIDING WITH AN ORGANIZED GROUP

The official leader of the group is called the trail boss and is usually a licensed guide whose experience will assure you a safer ride. Follow his instructions at all times, but don't be afraid to question anything you don't understand. He is there to help you and to prevent accidents.

When starting your ride, count the number of people in your group, and keep a running tally during the day. If anyone is missing, notify the trail boss at once.

Prevent accidents by watching the rider in front of you. For instance, if he pushes aside an overhanging branch, make sure it doesn't swing back and hit you or your horse. Similarly, if you are aware of any oncoming danger, warn the rider behind you.

In general, follow the rules for riding in company. Remain with your group at all times, and keep to the proscribed gait. Never wander off alone unless you are specifically told to do so, and never indulge in practical jokes or horseplay. Keep a horse's length behind the horse in front of you, and never touch another rider's horse.

Be courteous—signal if you plan to pass another rider and permit others to pass you. Do not, however, pass the lead rider or fall behind the drag rider. When tying your horse, keep him out of trouble by tying him a good distance away from other horses.

JUMPING SAFELY

Don't start to jump until you have acquired a strong, independent seat and have learned to control your horse properly.

Don't try to teach yourself. Begin by taking lessons from a professional instructor. Later, when you have learned the fundamentals, you can work on your own.

School on a steady, dependable horse who already knows how to jump and needs little direction. Always wear your safety hat and have someone standing by in case of accident.

Begin with modest jumps so you don't become frightened. In jumping, as in other forms of horsemanship, confidence is necessary for success. If you lose yours at the first rail, you may have a hard time regaining it.

To aid your balance in the beginning, buckle a narrow neck strap (this can be a stirrup leather or a martingale) about a foot above your horse's withers, and hold on to either side of it when approaching and jumping a fence. This will prevent you from grabbing the horse's mane and will keep your hands in the correct jumping position.

When jumping, never interfere with the horse's mouth by pulling back on the reins. If you feel you are falling and have not provided yourself with a neck strap, hang on to either the pommel (of the saddle) or the mane. Almost anything is better than disturbing the horse's head, which must stretch forward for the jump.

Never attempt a fence that is beyond your capabilities (or your horse's). Time and prowess—not desire—should determine the height of your jumps.

When jumping, always consider the effect of the terrain on your horse's legs and on his footing in general. Try to keep off hard, slippery surfaces, and don't make a habit of jumping down hills. When schooling him over fences, protect his legs with bell boots and shin and ankle boots.

If your horse is continually refusing fences and jumping poorly, don't chastise him—find out the reason why. It may be that he is lame or out of condition or that a piece of saddlery is painful to him. If none of these is the case, the fault may very well be yours. Get a professional opinion.

If you erect a series of fences, place them in a circle, not in a straight line. The former will keep your horse jumping at a steady pace; the latter will stir him up.

Vary the fence—and your approach to it—so your horse does not lose interest in his work.

Always end your session on a positive note. Stop after a good jump and give your horse a small reward. If you finish badly and let him know you are displeased, you may discourage him from trying again next time.

SHOWING YOUR HORSE

PREPARING TO SHOW

Plan your horse's show schedule carefully. Don't overbook him. If you keep him in the ring all year round, you will shorten his showing life. Showing is hard work, and even the strongest horse will wear down under constant pressure.

Once you decide to enter a show, fill out your entry blank and send it in as soon as possible. Horse shows are so popular today that many classes are filled six to eight weeks before the show actually takes place.

Enter a class that is right for you and your horse, one that is compatible with your training and experience. Don't get in over your head.

If you enter two or more classes, space them well apart so that your horse gets a chance to relax between performances. Don't overexert him.

Find out whether or not your horse is required to have a Coggins test for equine infectious anemia (swamp fever). In many states, a negative test is mandatory for all show horses, and violation of the law involves heavy fines and possible imprisonment.

When filling out your entry blank, make sure the information contained in it is absolutely correct. Any misrepresentation of fact, even an accidental one, can cost you a ribbon and make you liable for further penalty.

After your entry has been accepted, double check the requirements of your particular class and make sure you understand all the rules.

Make sure you are properly turned out for your class. Wear clothes that are clean, comfortable, and in good condition.

Inspect your tack, clean it, and make sure it, too, is in good condition. When you arrive at the showgrounds, there will be many things to keep you busy—you will need to unload your trailer, feed and water your horse, groom, etc. Preparing your equipment in advance will leave you more time to concentrate on your performance.

Protect your horse from contagious diseases by bringing your own feed and water buckets to the show. If possible, bring your own feed, also. Community feed boxes and watering troughs are great germ repositories and can be hazardous to your horse's health.

Be prepared for minor emergencies by bringing along the following:

- Insect repellent
- Aspirin
- Band-Aids
- Needles, thread, and extra buttons
- Safety pins
- Hairpins, hair bands, hairnets
- Washcloth

- Ice cubes in a plastic bag, to cool you off in summer or to tend sprains and bruises
- Tissues, rags, paper towels, for cleaning, shining, wiping, and dusting off just about everything
- Raincoat or poncho, if the weather looks threatening
- Suntan oil, if the sun is strong

AT THE SHOW SITE

Plan to arrive about one and one-half to two hours before your class begins, so you can tend your horse without haste or anxiety.

When you arrive, go directly to the secretary's tent and check in. Make sure there have been no program changes and that your class will be held on schedule.

Take your horse on a tour of the ring and the showgrounds. If he balks at any object, allay his fears by giving him a closer look at it. A ride around the ring, if permitted, will benefit both of you. Your horse will learn what is expected of him, and you will learn the type of handling he requires from his reactions.

If it is your horse's first show, give him plenty of exercise to calm him down before his debut. Try to make him as comfortable and relaxed as possible. If he is excited, work him on a lunge line, but be sure to control him well so he does not upset other horses.

If you have any complaints about the way the show is being run, if there has been any violation of rules or any misrepresentation, file a protest with the show steward. He will do his best to straighten things out.

SHOWING SAFELY

Go to the collecting ring before your class is called so the steward can see that you are present. Follow the steward's instructions at all times; never argue with him.

Find out which way the course goes *before* you enter the ring. Enter the ring in a poised and confident manner and respond promptly to the judge's commands.

Try to maintain an even, flowing pace for the duration of the course.

Stay at least one horse's length behind the horse in front of you. Never crowd other riders or allow them to crowd you. This is particularly important at your first few shows, when your horse is unused to the excitement of the ring and to large crowds of people.

If your horse misbehaves, always reprimand him quickly and quietly. However, if he becomes exceptionally unruly, take him out of line until he calms down.

Always be courteous to other riders. Never push them out of the way to obtain a better position in front of the judge.

If, after a show, you wish to consult one of the judges, ask the steward for permission to do so.

Never be afraid to pull out of a show if you feel that you and your horse are in danger. If inclement weather has made the course slippery or unsafe or if you feel your horse is about to act up and you cannot control him, get the secretary's permission to withdraw. Do not, however, withdraw or leave the show-grounds without the secretary's permission, or you are apt to be penalized.

CARING FOR YOUR HORSE

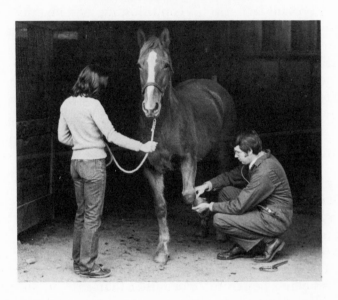

FEED

In his natural state, the horse was a grazing animal, unaccustomed to regular feedings. Though man has domesticated him and changed his life-style, he has been unable to change his eating habits. This is because the horse is a big animal with a very small stomach. Incapable of digesting large quantities of food at any one time, he satisfies his body's requirements by continually nibbling, and all diets and feeding schedules we impose on him today must be based on the life he led yesterday.

WHAT SHOULD A HORSE EAT?

A horse's basic diet consists of oats, hay, and grass. Supplements include corn, bran, vitamin concentrates, and certain approved vegetables. Exactly how much of these foods your horse receives will depend on his age, weight, and work. The one exception is hay. This is the mainstay of his diet, the single most important factor in his conditioning, and he must always be allowed as much as he can eat. Unlike grain, which is fed at regular intervals, hay should be available around the clock. Salt is another essential. It replaces body salts lost through sweating and should always be present in the stable or pasture. You can add a teaspoonful to your horse's feed or attach a salt lick to the stable wall.

HOW SHOULD HE BE FED?

If your horse is to develop good bones and strong legs, he must get plenty of vitamins and minerals. Ask your vet to help you plan a balanced diet. He will know which foods suit the animal's needs and temperament.

Buy high-quality hay and grain and store it in a dry, clean place. Good grain will be free of mold. Good hay will be crisp, sweet-smelling, green in color rather than brown, and free of dust. If it is discolored, you can assume it is moldy.

Feed your horse three times a day, if possible. His stomach is small and the more frequently he eats, the more comfortable he will feel.

Make sure there is always plenty of hay for your horse to munch on. Replenish his supply two or three times a day and always before going to bed.

Stick to a regular feeding schedule. Your horse is a creature of habit and he will be happier if he's fed at the same time every day.

Strike a good balance between food and work. A horse who works several hours a day will need more solid food (oats) than one who is idle.

Make sure your horse has clean feed buckets. Remove leftover food before it spoils or gets moldy.

Avoid feeding practices that lead to colic. The number one

horse killer in America today, colic is a digestive ailment brought on by dietary abuse. The stomach fills up with gas, the gas puts pressure on the lungs and the result is heart failure. You can prevent it by following these rules:

1. Never feed your horse when he is overheated or excited.
2. Never let him work right after he eats.
3. If you change his diet, do so gradually, over a period of days.
4. Never let him overeat. If you feed him more food than he can work off, fat will accumulate around his body and eventually around his vital organs. Even if he doesn't grow colicky, he will be unable to perform properly.

WATER

When a horse goes without food, several days can pass before there is a notable change in his appearance. When he goes without water, he will thin down in a matter of hours. Water is absolutely essential to a horse's well-being, and he must have a good supply on hand at all times. Even though he drinks very little—maybe three buckets a day—he will grow frantic if he is denied his ration. Follow these rules:

1. Make sure your horse's water is fresh and clean. Fish out any food or foreign matter that has fallen into it.
2. Water your horse first thing in the morning, last thing at night, and at least once in between. Check his water bucket regularly to make sure it isn't empty. If he is allowed to drink at will from a large trough, make sure the water is changed daily. In summer, when it can stagnate, it should be changed more frequently. In winter it should be checked for ice.
3. Water your horse *before* you feed him. If you water him after meals, you can wash the undigested food right out of his stomach. *Note:* After watering, let some time elapse before you feed. Once your horse learns that feed follows water, he will sacrifice the appetizer for the main course.
4. Never water your horse when he is hot; cool him down first.

5. Keep your horse away from stagnant ponds. If he drinks from a river or stream, make sure its banks are not steep and slippery and its water is not polluted or sandy. Sand can accumulate in the stomach and cause colic.

EXERCISE

Exercise is as vital to a horse as food and water. Without it, his muscles go slack, his body grows fat, and his belly gets so large that it crowds his lungs and impairs his breathing. If you ride him in this condition, he will pant and heave and sweat profusely. If you push him too far, he may become seriously ill. Clearly, this is too sad a fate for any animal, and you can prevent it by giving him the exercise he needs to keep fit.

Give your horse at least an hour's exercise per day. Two hours are even better. If he is lame or cannot be ridden, lead him out for about twenty minutes daily.

Exercise your horse according to his needs. Young horses and broodmares can be exercised in the pasture, but a horse that is ridden needs to walk and trot for several miles on a trail or bridle path. *Note: walk* and *trot;* the faster paces have no value as exercise and, if treated as such, can do more harm than good.

If your horse is out of condition, do not trot, but concentrate on walking for about a week. Altogether, it will take six weeks of proper food and exercise to get him fit again.

If your horse is working—and by "working" we mean showing, hunting, schooling, racing, trail riding, or any other activity in which more than average effort is required—his work schedule will determine the amount of exercise he needs. For instance, if he works several times a week, he needs little exercise on his days off. If he works once a week or less, he needs a full quota of exercise to keep him fit between engagements. In either case, a day of rest should follow a long day of work. *Caution:* If your horse refuses to eat, limps, or seems out of sorts, don't let him work. Call your vet immediately.

Never overtax your horse. Build him up with proper exercise before you ride him hard or work him. If he has not been ridden much during the winter, don't rush his spring training. Condition him slowly. Overexertion is a major cause of unsoundness, particularly in young horses.

Don't expect your horse to exercise himself. If you leave him in a ring or pasture, he will spend most of his time standing, playing, or nosying about. Unless you ride or lunge him, he will not get the exercise he requires.

HEALTH

The modern horse requires more care than any other animal man has domesticated. His health is constantly being threatened, not because he is a weak, frail creature, but because his current life-style differs so markedly from his natural one and because his new environment is filled with dangers he is not physically or psychologically equipped to handle. For these reasons, the job of protecting him belongs to you. And though it is a big one, you will find that vigilance and common sense prevent most injuries and diseases.

PROPER VETERINARY CARE

Every horse should be checked by a qualified veterinarian at least once a year. He should be inoculated against disease and examined thoroughly for any condition that could hinder his performance, impair his functioning, or endanger his life. For most horses, checkup time comes in the early spring, when they and their riders emerge from the winter doldrums and begin to prepare for the riding and showing season ahead. In nine out of ten cases, lack of sun and green grass will have robbed them of vitamins; lack of exercise will have made them fat; and lack of company will have left them bored. It is the ideal time for a good going-over, and you can make the vet's job easier by noting any changes in your horse's habits—eating habits particularly—or appearance. Such changes are usually the first signs of illness, and the sooner your vet hears about them, the sooner he can begin treatment. In this way, minor problems cannot turn into major ones.

Shots and Vaccinations

When scheduling these, remember that some vaccines need six to eight weeks to confer full immunity. If you are priming your horse for a show, plan accordingly. Most vaccines are effective for a year, then require boosters.

All horses need protection from tetanus, a fatal infection caused by contaminated cuts and puncture wounds, and from encephalomyelitis, sleeping sickness. There are three forms of the latter disease: VEE (Venezuelan encephalomyelitis), EEE (eastern encephalomyelitus), and WEE (western encephalomyelitus).

Horses who compete in shows and other group events need protection from distemper (or strangles), a throat infection contracted directly from other horses, or indirectly from common watering troughs and feeders. They also need protection from influenza, a respiratory infection spread by direct and indirect contact.

Broodmares need protection from rhinoneumonitis, an abortion-causing virus most frequently found on breeding farms.

Horses who suffer from various types of staph and strep infections may need special shots.

Note: Although there is at present no vaccine for equine infectious anemia (EIA or swamp fever), the Coggins test is a simple, inexpensive way to find out whether or not your horse has this deadly disease or is a carrier of it.

Worming

Internal parasites are the worst enemies your horse can have. Besides making him anemic and sluggish, they can cause colic and can damage his liver, lungs, and intestines. Make sure he has a professional worming several times a year to keep up his energy and to help him get the most out of his food.

Dental Care

There are two reasons for checking your horse's teeth at least once a year. One, because of the way he chews, the outside edges of his upper teeth become very sharp and, unless they are filed down or "floated," he will develop sores in his mouth. And two, because one bad tooth may stop him from chewing and cause him to swallow his food whole. This will interfere with his digestion and, even if he does not get sick, he will lose the nutritional benefits of his meal.

ELIMINATING GERMS

Try to keep your stable free of insects, rodents, and other disease-carrying pests.

To kill bacteria and prevent disease from spreading, disinfect every piece of equipment, every stall, and every vehicle that has been in contact with a sick horse. Put the horse himself in isolation and make sure other horses have no direct contact with him. Above all, don't let them share his feed bucket or water trough. If any of them have had direct or indirect contact with him, they too should be isolated.

If you buy a new horse, keep him away from your other horses until you are sure he is not carrying a contagious disease. Provide him with separate housing and pastureland for twenty-one days, and don't let him "visit" over fences. Have your vet give him a thorough going-over, and be on the lookout for any suspicious symptoms. When his probationary period has passed and he has joined the other horses, disinfect the stall and equipment he used in isolation.

THE IMPORTANCE OF SHOES

When a horse is working or being ridden on hard surfaces, he needs metal shoes to protect his hooves from injury and wear. Have him shod every five to eight weeks (the time will vary with the horse) by a professional blacksmith, and pick his feet out at least once a day. When doing so, make sure the shoes continue to fit properly and are in good condition. If they grow too thin, come loose, or are lost, replace them immediately. Bad shoes can ruin your horse's feet and affect his health. Follow these rules:

1. Never put off your visits to the blacksmith. If you leave shoes on too long, the walls of the hooves grow out over them, encouraging corns and causing the horse to stumble.
2. If you turn your horse out for any appreciable length of time, remove his shoes. A horse at grass should be barefoot. However, his hooves will still need trimming and he should see a blacksmith regularly.

PREVENTING LAMENESS

Your horse can become lame from working when he is too young, working at a job he is not qualified to do, or working too hard.

Don't be in a hurry to start him riding or showing. He should not be ridden until he is three years old, and then schooling should be confined to basics. Specialized training—jumping, roping, cutting—can begin when he is four, but until he is five, his body will not be able to withstand the rigors of competition.

Make sure he is physically qualified for the job at hand. In the end, conformation determines a horse's fitness for his work. No matter how good his reflexes, no matter how great his coordination or his motivation, he will ultimately break down if his body is not built to withstand stress or if his legs are not angled to withstand concussion.

Don't push him too far. Activities like jumping and racing put great strain on a horse, and if he is overworked, he can easily go lame. Remember, too, that sudden strain produces torn ligaments and muscles. Be sure to give him a good warm-up before you ask him to do hard work.

HEALTH RECORDS

It is not always easy to remember when your horse had his distemper shot, when he last saw the blacksmith, or when he was wormed. Keeping a written account of his medical history and jotting down important dates will help you, and the vet, take better care of him. Your file should also note his *normal* temperature, pulse, and respiration rates, so that if he gets sick, you will have a basis of comparison.

SYMPTOMS OF ILLNESS

Always be alert to changes in your horse's behavior and appearance, but remember that one symptom can have many different meanings. If your horse shows any sign of the following, call your veterinarian. He alone is qualified to diagnose and prescribe.

Partial or Complete Loss of Appetite

Most horses are avid eaters, and any loss of interest in food usually means that something is wrong. However, the problem may be a dental one. If he is not chewing his food or is chewing only on one side of his mouth, have his teeth examined immediately.

Temperature

A horse's normal temperature will range from 99 degrees F. to 101 degrees F. (foals run a little higher). Anything above 101 degrees F. needs to be investigated.

To take your horse's temperature, use either a veterinary or human thermometer lubricated with petroleum jelly. Insert it into his rectum and hold it in place (for three minutes), or else tie it to his tail with a piece of string so it doesn't get lost. If it disappears into his rectum, don't try to extricate it. It will be passed in a bowel movement.

Rapid Breathing

The normal rate is twelve to twenty-one breaths per minute with occasional pauses in between. In illness, there will be no pauses, and the rate will rise to thirty or more breaths per minute.

To get your horse's respiration rate, observe the rise and fall of his rib cage or listen at his nostrils. If you hear a "rattling" sound, he may have lung or respiratory problems.

Rapid Pulse

Thirty-six to forty-eight beats per minute are normal. Sixty or more indicate pain or overexertion.

To take your horse's pulse, feel the artery in his heavy jaw muscle or press your ear to the left side of his chest. Pulse should be taken only when a horse is at rest, never when he has just come in from work.

Bad Breath

A horse's breath normally smells somewhat like his feed. Foul odor may indicate colic, sinusitis, or tooth trouble.

Lameness

A lame horse will bob his head to the side when he walks, and the direction he bobs it in will tell you which leg is sore. He will bob his head away from a lame foreleg but toward a lame hind leg.

Other Symptoms

- Diarrhea, constipation, or any change in feces or color of urine
- Scratching or itching
- Lumps or swellings
- Sweating, coughing, runny nose
- Pawing, rolling, listlessness, stiffness
- Dull coat, hair loss

SAFETY IN THE STABLE

STABLE DESIGN AND CONSTRUCTION

Good stable design protects the rider, protects the horse, and protects the stable itself *from* the horse. Whatever the size or style of your facility, make sure it is strong, well ventilated, and free of hazards. Above all, make sure it has plenty of accessible fire exits.

If you need help in stable planning, expert advice is readily available in nearly every state. Just call your local Cooperative Extension, listed in the telephone directory under United States Government, Department of Agriculture, and ask to speak to the county agricultural agent.

BUILDING SITE

The location of your stable is important to your horse's health and to your own convenience. A few simple factors can make the difference between a building that works well for you and one that never seems quite right:

- Make sure your stable is within easy reach of your home and of a service road. This will facilitate the delivery of food and supplies and will make your horses accessible in all kinds of weather.
- Build on high ground so that water drains *away* from your stable. Avoid hollows where water will accumulate and freeze in the winter.
- Build on ground with good natural drainage, such as chalk or gravel. Avoid clay, which retains water and creates special drainage problems.
- Choose a site that is airy without being drafty. If your stable is hemmed in by trees and other buildings, it will not get enough fresh air; on the other hand, if it sits on an exposed hilltop, it will be buffeted by winds. Both alternatives are equally objectionable.
- Have the doors and windows of your stable face south so that your horses are protected from northerly and easterly winds.

BUILDING MATERIALS

Any structure that houses your horse must be strong enough to endure the kicking, biting, and occasional cussedness of a one-thousand-pound animal. Brick and concrete are best suited to the task—and they are fireproof—but wood is acceptable provided it is at least two inches thick and very hard. (Oak is best, plywood is *out*.) Metal prefabs are available, but these resound when kicked, and often dent.

Caution: If you use sheet-metal siding, make sure it is lined with two-inch oak and is installed and maintained properly so your horse cannot get his foot under it or through it.

SIZE

The standard stall is twelve feet square. Stallions, large horses, and mares with foals need more spacious quarters, about fourteen to sixteen feet square. Ponies, yearlings, and weanlings can do with smaller stalls, about ten feet square.

A stall should have a high ceiling and doorway, to provide adequate ventilation and to allow the horse sufficient head room. If your ceiling is under nine feet tall, your horse may hit his head on it if he rears. If it can't be raised, it should be padded. Low-hanging beams, of course, are taboo.

FLOORS

Stall floors must be firm enough to support your horse but not hard enough to hurt his legs. They must be able to withstand pawing and digging, must be smooth enough to prevent slipping, and must provide good drainage. Most materials have their advantages and their drawbacks, so the choice is pretty much yours: wood is easy to maintain but expensive; clay is desirable but requires work; concrete and asphalt are cheap but hard and also slippery when wet. Also remember that although stall floors are generally sloped a bit for proper drainage, the slope should be minimal so your horse need not fight to maintain his balance.

Aisle floors are usually brushed concrete or asphalt. Although dirt provides a better surface, it creates dust and is difficult to contain.

Bedding is important for drainage and provides a warm, comfortable, and sanitary place for your horse to lie down. It also protects him from bedsores, which come from sleeping on hard ground, and shoe boils, which are caused by a horse banging his elbow on the heel of his shoe when he is lying down.

Bedding should be freshened daily and should always be abundant, so your horse will not slip and injure himself when getting up. Many varieties are available:

● Straw: very absorbent but expensive and hard to dispose of.

● Wood shavings: inexpensive, readily available, and probably the most popular. However, make sure it does not
contain large chips of wood that will injure your horse if
swallowed.
● Sawdust: also popular because of its price and avail-
ability. Remember, though, that it heats up when wet and
must be changed frequently.
● Sand: has the advantages and disadvantages of a beach:
it's comfortable in warm, dry weather, cold and damp
when the weather turns. If you use it, make sure it
doesn't come from a saltwater beach. Horses like to lick
salt and too much sand in the stomach will cause colic.

VENTILATION

Horses are well equipped to deal with cold but are extremely
sensitive to wind. Therefore, the best shelter is one that elimi-
nates drafts but allows fresh air to circulate freely in all types of
weather. Three precautions:

1. Avoid low-level windows that allow air to blow directly
   on your horse. Always install windows high up in the
   stable and make sure they fit well, close properly, and are
   adequately weathered. If windows must be set at a low
   level, use small panes of glass and protect them with wire
   mesh or iron bars. Wherever possible, place windows on
   opposite walls to ensure cross-ventilation.
2. Never let your stable turn into a steambath. If it gets too
   hot, use fans to cool it down.
3. If you install heat, use it sparingly. When a horse goes
   outdoors from an overheated stall, he stands a good
   chance of acquiring a respiratory infection.

DOORS, PARTITIONS, AND HARDWARE

Doors have two functions: to keep the horse inside the stall and
to keep him from leaning into the aisle and nipping at people
and other horses.
   Doors must be four to five feet wide and not less than eight
feet high so the horse can pass in and out without knocking

himself. They must be solidly built to withstand rough usage and should be placed to the side of the stall so the horse can stand clear of drafts.

Depending on your needs and taste, you may choose either Dutch doors, sliding doors, or solid doors topped by mesh. Sliding doors have two advantages—they keep stable aisles clear and are free of troublesome hardware. However, if you use hinged doors, make sure you hang them so they open into the *aisle*, not into the *stall*.

Partitions are usually made of solid wood, bars, or mesh. Holes in the mesh and spaces between bars must never be large enough to entrap legs, and all protrusions must be eliminated to prevent snagging and scratching.

Partitions should be at least seven feet high so horses cannot straddle them or nip each other through them. However, the top three feet should be made of a see-through material so that these gregarious animals can satisfy their need for company.

Hardware constitutes one of the biggest of all stable hazards. Make sure all your nails, hinges, and latches are the heavy-duty kind, and fasten them securely so they cannot pull out. Mount them flush to their supports so they don't protrude, and position them so they can't scratch your horse when he walks through a doorway.

A safe stable. Note high window, protective metal cage over lightbulb, fire extinguisher, and equipment hung neatly on wall, leaving the aisle free of clutter.

ELECTRICITY, LIGHT, AND WATER

Good lighting is important in a stable. When you see clearly, you work better and are less likely to make mistakes or hurt yourself. However, good lighting depends on electricity, and electricity often means danger. To avoid shocks and fires, monitor all stable fixtures and appliances carefully. Encase all light bulbs in heavy metal grilles or cages and do not allow hot bulbs to come in contact with dry hay or straw. Make sure all wires are in metal conduits so they cannot be chewed or stepped on. Keep all electrical outlets in good working order and make sure water tank heaters are properly grounded.

Water faucets should be located *outside* the stalls so that humans can reach them easily but horses cannot. When needed, water can be drawn into the stalls with a short hose. Use frost-free faucets that won't freeze up in winter.

ACCESSORIES

Buy sturdy feed and water buckets that will not crush or dent easily. Check them for sharp edges and jagged rims, and if possible, remove the handles so your horse will not get a leg caught in them.

Caution: Never convert old tires or used furniture into feed tubs. If your horse swallows indigestible bits of rubber, nylon, or wood, he can ruin his stomach.

Mangers—iron or wooden troughs mounted flush to the wall of your horse's stall—are the safest of the hay feeders. If you don't have one, stack your horse's hay on an unused portion of his stall floor. Avoid hay nets and overhead hayracks. They can easily trap a foot or a halter, and the dust they produce is irritating to the horse's eyes and throat.

ELIMINATING STABLE HAZARDS

The old saying "If a horse can find trouble, he will" is perhaps truer in a stable than anywhere else. Stables offer marvelous opportunities for misadventure, and in order to make yours a safe place for you and your horse, you must choose the right equipment, keep it in good repair, and eliminate hazards from your daily routine.

Enforce stable security, so your horse cannot get loose and run away. Make sure all stable doors and gates are kept closed.

Keep your stable free of debris. There should be no tin cans, loose nails, broken glass, or bits of wire lying about to injure your horse.

Keep stable aisles free of clutter. Tack, tack stands, trunks, stools, and equipment belong in the tack room, not in passageways.

Check stable floors, walls, doors, and gates regularly for loose boards and protruding objects. Make sure all locks, hinges, hooks, and fixtures are securely nailed to their supports.

Store all food and grain in a dry, clean place so it does not get moldy. Keep the door to the storage room locked, so your horse cannot break in. If he does, he will overeat, and overeating can kill him.

Place your horse's feed and water buckets in an unused corner of his stall so he doesn't knock them over. Place them at a convenient height so he can reach them easily.

Remove soiled bedding and manure daily, then sweep stalls thoroughly. Droppings are a health hazard. If left to fester, they attract flies, spawn parasites, and spread disease.

Keep all poisons locked up and away from food. Never use a spray or an insecticide without first reading the label on the can.

Be prepared for accident and injury. Keep first-aid equipment within each reach.

Avoid mistakes and duplications in your stable routine. Post your feeding, watering, and work schedules on a bulletin board for all hands to see. Specify how much feed each horse is to receive. Note all changes in procedure or any special instructions. List all important telephone numbers—veterinarian, blacksmith, saddle shop, feed supplier, and fire department.

FIRE PREVENTION

To anyone who loves and keeps horses, a stable fire is the ultimate catastrophe. Even when lives are not lost, the emotional toll is high. To spare yourself unnecessary heartache, take a good, hard look at your stable and eliminate trouble spots. Ask yourself the following:

Does your stable have enough fire exits? Is it protected by lightning rods? Smoke detectors? Is it well ventilated, or can heat and dangerous fumes build up inside it?

Have you posted the telephone number of your fire department where everyone can see it? Do you know where your fire alarms are located? Where water is located?

Do you have a fire extinguisher that works? Is it within easy reach? Do you know how to use it?

Do you refrain from smoking in the stable and forbid anyone else to do so? Is there a "No Smoking" sign in plain view? Remember that hay and bedding are highly flammable and require only a small spark to set them ablaze. To be safe, store them outside the stable in a separate enclosure. The same goes for manure and combustibles like paint, turpentine, gasoline, and floor and wall adhesives. If outside storage is impossible, see that your storage area is separated from your stable by a fire-resistant wall and that it has fire-resistant, self-closing doors. That way, if a fire does start, you will be able to contain it more easily.

Did you know that, in addition to being highly flammable, hay, grain, feed, and manure heat and ignite spontaneously? If your hay is damp on the surface and has a fruity odor, you have a potential fire on your hands. Take the temperature of the hay by lowering a pipe several feet into it, and then sending down a thermometer on a string. If the thermometer registers above 160 degrees F., call the fire department at once.

Do you check all electric wires, outlets, and fixtures regularly? Is your wiring adequate for your needs? When you install new electrical equipment, do you make sure your wiring can handle the extra load? Is your wiring done by a licensed electrician?

Do you prohibit the use of hot plates and other heating units in and around your stable? When you use electric groomers and clippers, do you keep the wires high, so they are beyond your horse's reach? Do you disconnect all extension cords when you are no longer using them?

Do you have a security system that prevents outsiders and

unauthorized personnel from entering your stable when you are not on the premises? As you can see from the chart, arson is one of the major causes of fire.

Do you know how to get your horse out of a burning stable? Horses are so afraid of fire, they will not leave their stalls—even to save their lives. To make your horse move out, cut him loose, then cover his head (but not his nostrils) with a jacket or towel so he cannot see the flames. Lead him out, then make sure he gets plenty of air. If he looks unwell, call the vet immediately. Horses are extremely sensitive to smoke and can become dangerously ill from inhaling too much of it.

Have you ever had a fire drill? When fire starts, time is your greatest enemy. You have only a few seconds to act—to put out the blaze or lead your horses to safety. Knowing what to do and how to do it quickly can save precious lives. The fire department recommends that you follow this procedure whenever fire begins:

1. Call the fire department.
2. Begin evacuating horses.
3. Open all outside access gates to the stable area.
4. Keep roads clear for fire department access.
5. Use first-aid fire fighting equipment, such as hand extinguishers, buckets, etc.
6. Meet the fire department apparatus and direct it to the fire.

According to the National Fire Protection Association, a recent five-year period produced 29,100 stable fires, representing an estimated loss of $82,240,000. The causes of those fires were listed in this order:

CAUSE	PERCENT OF FIRES
Heaters	23
Electric wiring or apparatus	18
Careless smoking	18
Arson	11
Children and matches	6
Spontaneous ignition of hay	5
Lightning	5
Torches—plumber's, welder's, etc.	4
Hot plates	3
Friction	3
Sparks from flues or rubbish	3
Exposure	1

The Association firmly believes that almost without exception, a stable owner can "substantially reduce the possibility of fire by applying common sense rules of fire prevention."

SAFETY
IN THE
PASTURE

Choose fencing that will not cut or scratch your horse. The post and rails combination is safest, but wire is okay too, provided it is not barbed wire.

Start your fence two to two-and-one-half feet off the ground, to keep your horse from cutting his leg on it when he paws the ground. Set the upper rails close together, or else string some wire between them, so he can't poke his head through and rub out his mane.

Make sure your pasture includes some shade, so your horse does not fry in the sun. If your land has no trees, build him a small shelter where he can escape the flies that plague him in summer.

Before you turn your horse loose in a pasture, remove his halter. When scratching, he is apt to catch a hoof in it.

If you take your horse to a new pasture, give him a guided tour of the premises before you allow him to run free. Show him where to find the things he needs, and point out all obstacles and fences. A horse can be so distracted by other horses that he becomes oblivious of his surroundings. If this happens on unfamiliar territory, he may run smack into posts and wires without seeing them.

If you change your horse's environment in any way, do so in daylight when he can see what is happening. If you add new fences or reposition old ones, decorate them with long strips of cloth to attract his attention to the new arrangement.

Teach your horse to come to hand, so that he is available when needed. Begin by visiting him with some kind of treat. Stroke him gently while he nibbles, but make no attempt to catch him. Then walk away. When you repeat the tactic several days in a row, chances are he will be so amazed by your lack of aggression that he will come right to you. A word of advice: If he runs away from you, *never, never* run after him—you will only make him run faster. When he stops of his own accord, and he will, you can approach him again.

If your horse gets caught in a fence, try to prevent him from thrashing about so he does not cause himself further injury. Subdue him with the twitch or with any body hold that will keep him under control while you work him free.

Remember that lightning tends to strike the highest object in a field. Whenever an electrical storm begins, move your horse away from fences, poles, and trees that are likely to be hit.

Properly constructed pasture fence

PASTURE HAZARDS

Remove all low-hanging branches, beams, and projections.

Never use poisonous sprays on grass or shrubbery.

Beware of poisonous plants like yew, ragwort, and deadly nightshade. If any of these grow on your property, make sure your horse has no access to them.

Remove manure daily. Your horse will not graze in a field filled with droppings.

Note: Although it will not harm sheep, cattle, or crops, horse manure can infect horses and is never used to fertilize their pastureland.

Never leave shovels, rakes, or hoes lying on the ground. If your horse steps on one, its handle can jump up and strike him in the face or abdomen.

Pick up all debris. If your horse steps on, or plays with, bits of glass, metal, or wire, he will hurt his hooves; if he swallows them, he will cut his mouth or ruin his stomach.

HORSE THIEVES

Because riding is so popular today, the value of horses has increased considerably, and unfortunately so has the number of horse thieves. These people operate in several ways: Sometimes the horse is stolen outright; sometimes another horse, of inferior breed and quality, is substituted. The thieves' job is a simple one because today's horses are trained and trailer-broken early and are easy to catch. Thieves, however, are not so easy to catch and usually go free unless they are apprehended within two or three hours of the theft. If a horse owner is to recover his missing animals, he must be able to provide the police with an accurate and detailed description of them. To make sure you can provide such a description, keep a written record of your horse's whorls and cowlicks. Like human fingerprints, these are highly individual identity markers. They remain constant from birth and in no two horses will the type, size, and color be alike.

For further protection, you might also have your social security number—or some other number that only you would be likely to know—tattooed on the inside of the horse's flank, where it would not normally be visible.

RIDDING THE PASTURE (AND STABLE) OF FLIES

Fly control is important for three reasons. For one, flies and mosquitoes are the chief carriers of encephalitis and swamp fever. Second, horses who spend their time fighting flies fail to graze properly and are inadequately nourished. They are also apt to injure their bones and joints while tossing their heads, stamping their feet, and kicking at their bellies in an attempt to rid themselves of the nuisance. And finally, horses who are preoccupied with fighting flies cannot concentrate on their work and are unlikely to provide a safe or pleasant ride.

COMMERCIAL METHODS OF CONTROL

Foggers or Sprays

These are filled with insecticide and used to cover all interior and exterior surfaces, such as ceilings, walls, doorways, window frames, wooden fences, tree trunks, low-hanging branches, and, particularly, manure piles.

Vapona Resin Strips

These give off lethal vapors and are most effective in tightly closed buildings. They are hung from the ceiling, but must be placed out of the horse's reach if used in the stable.

Electronic Bug Killers

Used both indoors and out, these devices kill on contact and are incredibly effective in controlling all types of flying pests. However, when they snare a victim, they emit a loud noise which may be objectionable to many people—and horses.

Fly Repellents

These are applied directly to the horse's skin and come in a variety of forms, among them sprays, gels, sticks, handiwipes, and concentrates. All are helpful but must be used in moderation to avoid blisters and toxic effects. If you use a spray, show your horse how it works before you aim it at him. Then spray his least sensitive areas first (ankles, shoulders, etc.). *Never spray his head.* Use a handkerchief to apply repellent to his face, or else use a stick or a gel. When you ride, spray your horse just before you mount so he will be protected during your outing. If flies are especially numerous, buy him an ear net.

A note of caution about insecticides: Never forget that *all* insecticides contain dangerous chemicals and can be hazardous to your health if used incorrectly. To prevent accidents, follow these rules:

1. Always make sure you have the right product for the job at hand. Never use any insecticide without first reading the label.
2. Take all precautions suggested by the manufacturer.
3. Use only as directed. Increasing the dosage can have serious consequences.
4. When using concentrates, mix carefully and clean up all spills as soon as possible. If you leave puddles on the floor, your horse may lick them or someone may slip on them.
5. Cover your skin whenever you use a spray, and wash your hands thoroughly after you have finished.
6. Store all insecticides in a locked cabinet, and keep them away from food and out of the reach of children and horses.

NATURAL AND PRACTICAL METHODS OF CONTROL

Eliminate breeding grounds. Many flies lay their eggs in manure, straw, and wet hay. By cleaning your stable frequently and scattering these things in a reasonably distant field, you will eliminate one source of the problem.

Screen all doors and windows.

If possible, keep your horses in the stable during daylight hours, and turn them out when it gets dark. Flies are much less prevalent at night.

If you do turn your horse out during the day, try to pasture him on high, dry ground. The lower and wetter your land, the more flies it will attract.

Provide your horse with some good shade trees for protection. If this is not possible, build him a small shed or park your trailer in the field so there will be someplace he can go to free his head of face flies.

When you ride, do so in the early morning or early evening when it is cool and not quite so bright. Flies are most active in heat and bright sunlight. Also, remember to keep away from marshy areas and take along a fly switch for protection.

TRAILERING

THE TOWING VEHICLE

POWER

To pull a van that holds two horses, you will need aproximately 200 horsepower or, at the very least, a medium-sized car with a V-8 engine. A small foreign or compact car will not be strong enough to handle the load safely. If you are pulling four horses, you should have a light-duty pickup truck or a heavy-duty station wagon.

TIRES

Properly inflated, four-ply tires will provide enough stability for a one- or two-horse trailer. Larger vans require six-ply truck-type tires.

Caution: Be especially careful when driving with snow tires. Their treads are deeper than those of regular tires and will cause the trailer to wobble more than usual.

HITCH

Have your hitch installed in a shop that handles professional trailer hitches. They will make sure it is substantial enough to pull a horse trailer (some hitches, like bumper hitches, are too light for towing horses) and that it is the same height as the trailer tongue. If the heights of the tongue and hitch do not match, the weight of the trailer will rest in the wrong place and put undue strain on both car and trailer axles. The trailer will then sway badly, your tires will suffer, and your horse will spend the trip fighting to maintain his balance.

It is also a good idea to fit your trailer with load-levelers or equalizer bars. These keep the trailer riding level with the car and distribute its weight properly no matter how heavy a load it is carrying. They also prevent the trailer from jackknifing.

Once your hitch is installed, never take it, or any other part of your rig, for granted. Check it for rust or erosion before every trip, and immediately replace any metal that has been eaten away or shows signs of weakness.

Remember, too, that you can increase your safety and comfort by strengthening the overload springs in your car and adding heavy-duty shock absorbers.

THE TRAILER

BRAKES

Hydraulic brakes are safest because they operate independently of your car brakes and work normally, even if the car's electrical system fails. Electric trailer brakes, on the other hand, need to be hooked up to the car brakes—a major job—and are dependent upon them for power.

Brakes, in general, need to be checked at least once a year. If your trailer is new, check them after the first five hundred miles to make sure they haven't loosened. Brakes that grab are always dangerous and should be adjusted immediately.

TIRES

The rules for trailer tires are the same as those for car tires: well-inflated four-ply tires for a one- or two-horse trailer and six-ply truck-type tires for larger trailers.

BODY

A trailer must be wide enough and high enough to accommodate your horse comfortably and must be free of built-in hazards. The horse must have ample room to move, and all protruding objects must be eliminated.

Trailers, generally, have hardwood floors and sides, which need to be checked frequently for rot and replaced at the first sign of it. Any horse whose foot falls through a decaying floorboard can easily break a leg.

Although rotting is inevitable, there are many things you can do to slow down the process:

- Do not allow manure or moist bedding to remain in the trailer. Manure breeds bacteria, which, in turn, cause rotting; straw bedding pulls moisture from the air and causes rust as well as rot. After removing both these things, leave your trailer open in the back so it can air out and dry completely.
- Never install a new floor on top of an old one. Moisture will accumulate between the two and hasten the deterioration of both.
- Treat your floor with creosote once a year. It will make the wood last longer. Rubber mats which, keep the horse from skidding, also provide good protection.

The tailgates of the trailer must lock securely and be hinged properly to keep them from opening during your trip. If they do open, there is usually a safety chain or a solid tail bar behind the horse to keep him from backing out. Although the chain is more common, the bar is safer and more supportive. Horses like to sit on it and seem to draw confidence from it. However, if you are hauling two horses and have only one door on your trailer, you may need both devices so you can hold one horse while loading the other.

If your trailer has a solid partition down the center, make sure it is absolutely flush with the floor so your horse can't get his feet caught under it.

All trailers are different and some have more safety features than others. Although you are unlikely to find one that has everything, there are many handy devices you can install yourself, such as: a light inside the trailer, so you can keep an eye on your horse while driving at night or unloading in the dark; reflective tape on the back of the trailer, so other drivers can see it at night if your lights fail; and rings welded at important points inside the trailer and out, so you can tie your horse wherever it's convenient for you.

CAR AND TRAILER MAINTENANCE

Prevent rust by checking your trailer regularly for water seepage. Recalk leaking seams or joints from the outside with a latex calking compound, then paint them to match the color of the trailer.

Preserve the finish on your trailer by waxing it twice a year. A hard wax with a low silicone content will last longest.

Keep all electrical connections free of dirt and erosion, so trailer lights and brakes can work properly.

Check and lubricate your wheel bearings at least once a year.

Keep the hitch sleeve and all hinges and latches well oiled. Make sure the tail gate fittings are not cracked or broken. Replace worn tires immediately.

Remember that the older the trailer, the more it needs looking after. Keep a running check on all its crucial parts. Never be lax about making repairs or take chances with faulty equipment. If you buy a secondhand van, have a mechanic give it a thorough going-over. Your horse's life and your own depend on your vigilance.

DRIVING WITH A TRAILER

Learn everything there is to know about your trailer before hauling horses in it. Ride where the horses ride at least once, so you can feel how it takes bumps and turns, and absorbs shocks.

Join an automobile club that will come to your assistance whenever you run into trouble along the way. If possible, equip your car with a citizen's band radio. It will keep you up to date on road conditions, will warn you of potential danger spots, and will bring you help in a hurry in cases of emergency.

Check the trailer laws in your state, and make sure the van you are driving meets all its safety requirements.

Before setting off on a trip, make sure your entire rig is functioning properly. Examine your hitch and your safety chains. Check your brakes, lights, and turn signals. Check the air pressure in your trailer tires. If it's too low, you may be headed for a blowout.

Make certain all trailer doors are securely locked.

Drive in a smooth and steady manner. Start and stop slowly and take corners and curves at a speed your horse can negotiate easily. Never brake or swerve suddenly. Abrupt changes of speed can throw your horse off-balance and cause him grave injury.

Drive and park on pavement wherever possible. Your ride will be smoother and your tires will last longer.

Stay in the right-hand lane on turnpikes and superhighways.

Stop and check your horses and your trailer hitch at least once every hour. On long trips, take a rest break every three or four hours. Unload the horses so they can stretch their legs and work off cramps and stiffness. Always offer water, since some horses refuse to drink when riding.

When you reach your final stop, unload quickly. Horses should never be left in the trailer any longer than necessary.

THE TRAILER RIDE

A trailer ride is always a major event in a horse's life. Even if he shows no outward signs of stress, you must realize that he is under unusual pressures. Accosted by strange sounds and vibrations, he faces a situation that has disrupted his routine, circumscribed his movements, and possibly affected his digestive system. When caring for him en route, observe his mental and physical reactions to his new environment. Alert yourself to his needs, and make him as comfortable as possible. His behavior in a trailer may be very different from his behavior at home, and he may develop problems that require special handling. When dealing with these, always remember that he is an individual and needs to be treated with patience and understanding. Your efforts will be amply rewarded when you arrive safely at your destination with a fit and healthy animal.

GETTING READY

A safe trip begins long before you actually take to the road. Since travel can upset your horse mentally and physically, a little advance planning will save him needless pain and anxiety en route.

Give your horse plenty of time to get used to the van. Learning to load can be a traumatic experience for him, and it is important to get him over his fears before your trip begins. If you introduce him to the van long before you are actually ready to leave, you will prevent frazzled nerves and panic on departure day, and may even save his life. Far too many horses have been killed while fleeing confrontations at the loading site.

Choose a method of loading that is compatible with your horse's temperament. There are as many methods of loading horses as there are horses themselves. But unfortunately, none are infallible. A technique that drives one animal straight into the trailer is liable to send another running for the hills. Horses have their hangups just as people do, and each one's defense mechanism is different. Before you try any particular strategy, consider your horse's psychological makeup. Is he gentle? Or is he a kicker? Does he respond to coaxing, or will he need pushing? What sort of things upset him? Is he spooked by ropes? Brooms? Crops? Knowing him as you do, you can avoid methods that will distress or alarm him. Once frightened, he will put up a fight whenever he is asked to load, and his efforts to escape the van may end in tragedy.

Visit your veterinarian at least two months before the start of your trip. There are two important reasons for doing so:

1. Your horse must satisfy the health requirements of each state along your route. If his health certificate is not acceptable to local authorities, they will insist he be vaccinated at his point of entry. Since shots often have unpleasant side effects, this is a risk you cannot afford to take.
2. Some vaccines need six to eight weeks to confer full immunity. If you leave before the time is up, your horse may not be adequately protected against infection and disease.

Make sure your horse is in good health before you take him traveling. If he is not well, keep him at home until he recovers. Many minor ailments are aggravated by hauling and can become major problems on the road.

Prepare your horse for trailer living. If he normally drinks from a trough or creek, get him used to a bucket *before* you leave. A long-distance ride is not the time for innovations in diet or feeding methods.

WHAT TO TAKE ALONG

Feed

If you can pack enough for your entire trip without overloading your trailer and ruining your tires, do so. Your horse's regular feed may not be available en route, and a change of diet is always risky when traveling.

Equipment

Bring along the feed and water buckets your horse is used to.

The more familiar objects he sees, the happier he will be. Also, borrowed equipment is likely to contain the germs of other animals.

Bring several blankets. Climates vary from state to state, and you must be prepared for all types of weather.

Medications

Bring ointments and dressings for minor wounds and cuts, liniment for soreness and bruises, Vicks or Mentholatum for coughs and upper respiratory congestion, aspirin for pain, clean bandages and tape, and a knife to cut your horse loose if his halter rope becomes entangled.

Nervousness en route may cause constipation and digestive upset. If your horse is susceptible, your vet may want to quiet him down with tranquilizers; however, these should be administered only on the advice of a physician.

Bedding

All trailer floors should be lined with straw or wood shavings. Straw is better for three reasons: It is easier to keep clean, it doesn't blow around as much, and it acts as a shock absorber and protects the horse's legs. Unfortunately, horses tend to eat their bedding and you will have to prevent yours from overindulging if you want to avoid colic.

LOADING AND UNLOADING

Choose a safe place to load and unload. Avoid cluttered, closed-in areas and ground that is slippery or rocky.

When loading, have your horse wear a halter. *Only* a halter. Saddles, bridles, and other equipment will catch on trailer parts and make your job more difficult.

If a friend is helping you, make sure he knows your horse's idiosyncrasies. An animal with strong fears and aversions may react violently to some perfectly ordinary technique and cause injury to an unwitting assistant.

Always stand to one side when your horse is loading and

unloading. It is never safe to stand behind him or directly in front of him.

Never haul a stallion and a mare, or two stallions, in the same trailer. When a stallion travels with other horses, see that he is loaded first and unloaded last.

When carrying more than two horses, try to distribute their weight evenly in the van. If you are carrying one horse in a two-horse trailer, have him ride on the left-hand side.

Always fasten the tail bar behind your horse before you tie him in the van. When you unload, untie your horse first, then open all bars, chains, and doors.

CARING FOR YOUR HORSE EN ROUTE

Protective Devices

Good leg wrappings are essential to the safety of a grown horse. They protect him against self-abuse, bumpy roads, sudden stops, and the wear and tear of travel in general. Make sure you bandage all four legs. Start just below the knee, go down below the coronary band, over the bulb of the heel, then come up to the knee again. The bandages should contain several layers of cotton or other padding and should be wound smoothly and firmly so the horse cannot unravel them. If you have a chronic kicker, always apply a hock bandage to prevent capped hocks, and pad the inside of your trailer door.

Horse ready for trailering, with protective devices in place: leg wrappings, tail bandage, head bumper, goggles (necessary only when riding in an open trailer).

Cross-ties give your horse added support when traveling and improve his balance. They prevent him from getting his head around and keep him from biting and nipping other horses. If you provide a full haynet and enough rope to maintain a normal head carriage, your horse should not find them objectionable. However, if he is a fighter, it is probably safer to turn him loose and give him as much freedom as possible.

If your horse likes to lean on his tail, a tail bandage will keep him from losing hair and rubbing himself sore. The bandage should start at the point where the tail joins the body and should be about twelve inches long. It can be flannel, nylon, or double knit, but never elastic. Elastic bandages often grow too tight and should be avoided.

A head bumper will prevent your horse from being cut or bruised if you stop short. Goggles or a windshield will protect his eyes if he travels in an open vehicle.

Feeding and Watering

The strain of travel can slow down your horse's digestive system and even cause colic. Before you go, get your vet's advice on how to deal with upset stomach, constipation, diarrhea, and other problems. On departure day, feed your horse lightly about an hour before you leave. When traveling, try to keep to your normal feeding schedule. Stick to your horse's regular diet, but modify it according to climate and work load. A hard-working horse in a cold climate will require many more calories than an inactive one in a warm climate.

If your horse suffers from motion sickness, reduce the size of his portions but feed him more frequently. Try not to travel right after he has eaten.

A well-filled haynet placed within easy reach will keep most horses occupied and content during a long haul. Diverted by food, they are less likely to fight with each other and get into trouble.

Clean water is essential to your horse's health and appearance. Make sure it is always available to him. (If it isn't, he will thin down in a matter of hours.) If he drinks less than he should, or refuses to drink at all, make him thirsty by putting a little salt in his grain. Be careful, though, because too much salt can upset his stomach. If you know from past experience that your horse will not drink on the road, use a little gelatin powder to sweeten his water. Again, get him used to the new mixture at home before you offer it en route.

Great gulps of food and water are bad for your horse's digestive system, especially when he is traveling. Avoid situations that lead to overindulgence. Offer your horse water at every stop, so his thirst does not become overpowering. When filling his haynet, omit the kind of attractive tidbit that is quickly gobbled up.

Health Care

The ailments commonly associated with trailer travel are colic and lameness, swollen legs, cuts, bruises, and respiratory infections. Some of these are the result of loading and unloading, others come from nervousness, lack of exercise, and changes in schedule and diet. Whatever their source, it is a good idea to keep an eye out for symptoms and begin treatment as soon as possible. When you're far from home, professional help may be difficult to find. To locate a qualified vet, you may first have to find a local horseman (or stable) and ask for a recommendation.

When traveling, the temperature inside the van is as important as the temperature outdoors. To keep your trailer well ventilated, leave your windows open. Horses can adjust to cold, but heat makes them restless and subjects them to respiratory infection. This does not mean that blankets are taboo. By all means, blanket your horse in cold weather and blanket him against the wind, but check often to make sure he is not sweating.

Extremes of climate make good health care difficult. If your horse has a short, spring coat and goes from warm weather to cold, be sure he has extra blanketing. On the other hand, if he leaves the snow for the sunshine, be sure he is protected against heatstroke.

Cleanliness is essential to good health. Change your horse's bedding regularly. Don't encourage germs by allowing wastes to build up.

Behavior Problems

A restless horse who continually shifts his weight in the trailer can threaten the driver's control and make travel hazardous. If your horse begins to pace, he may be overtired or just plain stir crazy. Stop the car, walk him around a bit, and let him relax before you start up again.

Crosstying a horse and providing him with a full haynet should prevent him from biting and bothering his trailer mates. However, if you have several fighters in your midst, you may calm them down by rearranging their positions. Horses have their likes and dislikes just as people do, and some personalities are more compatible than others. Occasionally, you will get a horse who simply *cannot* quiet down, and he will have to be hauled separately.

Rests and Overnight Stops

Stop your van and check your horse at least once an hour. Take a rest break every three or four hours. When you break, unload your horse so he can stretch his legs and work off cramps and stiffness. Since he may not like to drink when riding, be sure to offer him water.

When you stop for lunch or breakfast, park your trailer in the shade. Never leave your horse to swelter in the sun.

On major highways, you can unload your horse and picnic in the official rest areas. While you're eating, tie your horse to the trailer and give him a bucket of water to play with.

Two things to remember: Keep him away from other travelers and clean up after him with a pail and shovel.

For overnight stays, try to find accommodations that adjoin an empty lot or field. Before checking in, ask the proprietor for permission to unload your horse. Half an hour's play at the end of a lunge line will refresh and relax him.

When choosing a place to stay, always consider your horse's comfort, and try to find him a spacious bed. Although he can sleep standing up, a night in a trailer will be hard on his legs and muscles. He will rest better and be better able to withstand the rigors of travel if he can move freely and lie down.

Before going to bed yourself, make sure he has a full bucket of water and plenty of hay. Always use your own buckets and your own feeding equipment. Common troughs at motels and stables are a great source of germs and disease.

When you reach your final destination, unload as quickly as possible. Never leave your horse in the trailer any longer than necessary.

Accidents

If you have a trailer accident, handle it as you do all other emergency situations—stay cool and don't panic. Try to help your horse but approach him carefully. Even if he is normally docile he is sure to be frightened, and his fear may lead him to kick and bite.

If your trailer has turned over, get your horse out *before* you right it, or you will cause him further injury. If you can, pull him out by his legs or his tail. A rope that avoids the bony parts will not hurt him.

BUYING
A HORSE

Before you buy a horse, make sure you know what is involved in *owning* one. Far too many animals suffer abuse and neglect at the hands of irresponsible owners who either fail to find out what is expected of them or are unwilling to put forth the necessary effort. Horsekeeping is hard work. And it is expensive. The price you pay to purchase your horse is only the first installment of a long-term obligation. Your horse must be fed, watered, groomed, stabled, exercised, and vetted properly if he is to survive. Any attempt to cut costs by providing inferior care will soon be evident in his appearance and performance, and can bring him to a tragic end. To prevent heartbreak—yours and his—never buy a horse unless you are physically, psychologically, and financially prepared to give him the necessities of life.

Purchase your horse from a reputable dealer. Many unsoundnesses are not visible to the untrained eye, and an unscrupulous trader will not hesitate to exploit your lack of expertise. In his efforts to con you, he can alter the horse's personality with tranquilizers or pep pills, file his teeth to make him look younger, or cover up cracks in his hooves with paint or mud.

Buy a horse that suits your purpose. Do you want a horse solely for pleasure riding? Trail riding? Endurance riding? Do you plan to compete seriously in horse shows? If so, in which class? Conformation, hunter, dressage? A horse who is totally unsuited to one type of work may be admirably fit for another. Make sure the horse you buy qualifies for the job you have in mind. However, be fair in your assessment of him. Don't make more demands than are necessary. If a pleasure horse is what you want, don't insist that he have the legs of a champion jumper. Defects that keep him out of the show-ring can be insignificant in the backyard.

Look your horse over carefully and learn to evaluate what you see. When buying a horse of your own, it is only too easy to be influenced by your emotions and to judge the animal on his charm rather than on his merits. However, by sticking to some common guidelines, you can make sure the horse you choose will be with you for a long time.

PHYSICAL CHECKPOINTS

LEGS

These are the most important parts of the horse's anatomy. If they are not sound, if they are weak or crooked, the horse himself will be of no value to you.

Check the horse's stance. Does he stand squarely? Does he toe in (pigeon-toed) or out (splay-footed)? If the former, he may have crooked legs or poor conformation. If the latter, his gait will be impaired.

Check the horse's feet. A misshapen foot or a dropped sole can be a sign of previous founder (acute inflammation of the laminae and sole) and can mean the horse is prone to that disease.

Note the positioning of the legs. Do the limbs appear to crowd each other? If so, the horse is probably "base narrow" and is prone to many kinds of unsoundness because he is forced to walk on the outside part of his hoof. A horse who is "base wide" also has problems. In his case, the space between his legs forces him to walk on the inside part of his hoof.

Examine the forelegs for: splints (bony growths between the splint bone and the cannon bone); cuts; sidebones (hard lumps on the side of the heel); ringbones (bony formations in the pastern); strained tendons; arthritis (soreness and swelling in the joints); and bursitis (inflammation of the joints).

Examine the hind legs for arthritis; bursitis; splints; curbs (thickening of the hock); cow hocks; knock-knees; spavin (bony growths below the hock joints); and stringhalt (a nerve disease causing one or both hind legs to jerk, and most noticeable when the horse backs).

Lumps, scars, and swellings on any leg need to be investigated. They can be serious or completely innocent, depending on how and when they were incurred and whether or not they affect the horse's gait.

Horse with lop ears, ewe neck, and parrot mouth

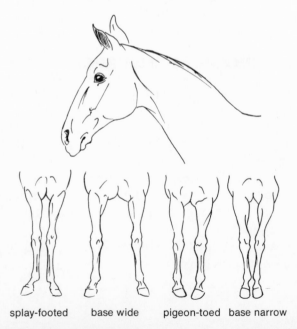

splay-footed   base wide   pigeon-toed   base narrow

THE EYES

Are both eyes the same size? Are they symmetrical? Does the horse blink in bright sunlight? If he doesn't, he is either totally blind or blind in one eye. Are the lids whole and in good condition? If they aren't, the eyes will be easily infected. Are they properly formed? If not, the horse may suffer from an eye disease.

THE NOSE

Check the nostrils for discharge and bad odor.

THE MOUTH

Does the horse have missing teeth or cavities? Do his teeth look as if they'd been filed down to conceal his age? Do his lips and tongue move normally? Are they in good condition? Do his upper teeth overhang the lower ones (parrot mouth)? If so, his jaw is malformed and he will suffer from digestive problems, because he cannot chew his food properly. Also, the condition may indicate other structural defects in the head.

THE EARS

Does the horse pick up his ears and look alert? If not, he may be deaf (stand away from him and snap your fingers to see if he hears), lop-eared (the ears droop forward or sideways, a defect in conformation classes), or just plain ornery. (Horses will lay back their ears just before bucking, rearing, etc.)

THE POLL

Look for poll evil—swelling or scars from a head collar or a blow. It may mean the horse was beaten.

THE NECK

Can the horse move his head freely? Does he heave (exhale twice after one breath) or roar (make noises when galloping because of abscesses in the throat)? Is the area between the poll and the withers convex? If it is concave, the animal is said to have an upside-down or a ewe neck, an undesirable quality.

THE WITHERS

Check for high withers, lumps, scars, and abscesses. The first means that the horse will not be able to carry much weight; the others, that he may be chronically afflicted with saddle sores.

OTHER

Look out for broken ribs, broken tails (ones that don't switch), hernias, and undescended testicles (in stallions).

After you have gone over your horse feature by feature, stand back and watch the way he moves. Does he have a straight and steady gait? Or does he limp, wing, or paddle (throw his front feet out)? Does he move easily and freely? Or does he seem sore and constrained? Is he well coordinated? Or are his movements rather haphazard? Does he have a long, smooth stride? If so, he will probably be easy to ride.

THE HORSE'S TEMPERAMENT

A horse who appears perfect in all other respects will sometimes exhibit vices that make him difficult, if not impossible, to live with. Before you make your final decision, ask yourself: Is your horse a cribber? (Does he grab railings and such with his teeth and suck in air at the same time?) Does he fight with most other horses? Is he easily bored? When nervous, does he kick apart his stall? Are there areas of his body that he will absolutely not let you touch?

Among horses, there is as great a variation in personality as there is among people. Because a horse belongs to a certain breed or is sound in every respect, it does not necessarily mean that he is right for you. In the end, you must choose a horse you are comfortable with, one whose temperament and character are compatible with your own.

OTHER CHECKPOINTS

PRICE

Make sure the price is right. Ask yourself: Does the cost of the horse accurately reflect his background and condition, or is it grossly out of line with both? Never pay for a thoroughbred when what you are clearly buying is a backyard horse. On the other hand, beware of the deal that looks too good—when an obviously superior horse is offered to you for virtually nothing. Chances are the animal is stolen or is unsound in some way that is not readily apparent.

A VET'S EXAM

Have your vet examine all prospective purchases. No matter how cheap a horse you are buying, no matter how many horses you have bought in the past, never agree to a sale until you have the animal in question checked out by a qualified veterinarian. What's more, the vet should be one that you, personally, have chosen. Never ask the seller to recommend a vet. Never use a vet in the seller's vicinity. And, above all, never use the seller's own vet. Doctors whom the seller has previously patronized may be reluctant to offend him with an unflattering report.

In the event that your own doctor is too far away to perform the examination, suggest that the horse be taken to a clinic associated with a nearby veterinary school. Under no circumstances agree to accept a previously issued health certificate as proof of the animal's current soundness and ability to perform. If the seller refuses to permit an on-the-spot examination, he is not to be trusted.

Finally, it is important to tell the vet how you plan to use the horse. That way, all defects can be put in their proper perspective.

Note: Sometimes, a horse who has been declared perfectly sound will go lame several days after an examination. This may be because the seller administered a pain-killing drug to mask the disability. If, during his examination of the horse, your vet suspects foul play, he should take a blood or urine sample to dispel his doubts.

ZONING LAWS

If you plan to keep your horse in your backyard or elsewhere on your premises, check your local zoning laws to make sure you have a legal right to do so.

INSURANCE

If you insure your horse against theft, injury, or death, make sure you read your policy through thoroughly, and understand all its terms. Go over every clause with your insurance agent so you know when and under what circumstances your horse is covered. While it is possible to insure a horse against almost every eventuality, there are stringent rules with which you must comply if you are to collect. For instance, some policies require you to obtain the written consent of both the insurance company and a licensed veterinarian before destroying (putting down) an injured horse.

BUYING A CHILD'S HORSE

Because of the youth and inexperience of the prospective rider, a child's horse needs to be chosen with extraordinary care.

Look for a dependable, easygoing animal with an even temperament. Geldings and mares generally have the gentlest dispositions. Stallions are completely out of the question.

Never buy an inexperienced horse for a child. The idea that horse and child can learn together is a highly dangerous one. To avoid confusion and frustration, a novice needs a trained mount who responds well to hand and leg signals and knows what is expected of him. Inevitably this raises the question of ponies. Many parents believe that, because of their size, ponies make ideal mounts for small children. Children, too, find them less threatening than horses, and certainly more appealing. Unfortunately, ponies tend to be unreliable—and for a very good reason: They are too small for any adult to ride or train and, consequently, they remain largely unschooled. Unless an exception can be found, most children are better off on a small horse.

Always buy the best horse you can. The sounder he is, the longer he will live. A child's pet is an emotional investment as well as a financial one, and the defective horse who comes to a tragic end and breaks its rider's heart is never a bargain. However, this does not mean you have to purchase a purebred animal in order to get a good mount. Unless your child plans to enter serious competition, a cold-blooded horse (mixed breed) is perfectly satisfactory.

Get to know the horse before you buy him. Watch how he behaves around children and around other horses. Observe him in the stable and in the pasture. Ask to ride him and question anything you don't understand or don't like. If you cannot get satisfactory answers to your questions or cannot observe and examine the horse at close range, don't buy him.

Don't buy at auctions unless you are an expert judge of horses. The choices may be wide and the prices low, but you will not get to examine the horse properly or really observe him in action.

After you buy your child a horse, make sure he learns to ride properly. Find a qualified instructor to undertake his training and see that he establishes the right relationship with his mount. Professional guidance is essential to a beginner. Putting a child (or an adult, for that matter) on an animal he does not understand and cannot control will undermine his confidence and frighten him away from riding. One fall is all it takes to make a child permanently afraid of horses, and this is truly sad when you consider that that fall need never have occurred.

RIDING
LESSONS

HOW TO FIND THE RIGHT INSTRUCTOR

If you are a beginner, with little knowledge of horses or riding facilities, look in the yellow pages of your telephone book for a list of stables in your area. Try to find out as much as you can about each facility, i.e., how long it has been in existence, what kind of reputation it has, whether it specializes in English or Western riding, whether or not it provides instruction, etc.

After you accumulate a reasonable amount of information, visit each facility and take a good look around. Ask yourself: Is the stable clean and orderly? Are the horses treated well? Do they look alert and healthy? Bored and listless? How do they react to the touch?

When you complete your tour of the premises, ask to sit in on a few lessons. Observe the relationship between the teacher and the students. Does each understand the other? Is the teacher's manner constructive and inspiring, or does it have an adverse effect on the students? Do the students look frustrated and upset, or do they seem happy with their progress?

After you visit a number of facilities and see the differences in management and approach, you should be able to choose a school that's right for you.

Most schools offer a choice of group or private lessons. Although the former are less expensive, be sure to find out the size of the group before you sign up for it. If it includes more than four people, chances are you will not get enough of the instructor's attention to warrant the price of admission.

When you are more advanced and have decided on the type of riding you want to do, you will need an instructor who specializes in your particular field. Unfortunately, such a person may not live in your immediate neighborhood. You may have to travel quite far to reach him, or he may have to come to you. In either case, travel expenses will be added to the price of the lessons, and your arrangements can become complicated. Before you enter into any agreement, make sure the terms are clearly spelled out. Always ask:

1. What is the price of the lessons? If you think it is too high, say so immediately. Then, you and the instructor can work out an equitable arrangement that will not bankrupt you or shortchange him.
2. How long are the lessons?
3. Where will the lessons take place? If they are not given on premises owned by you or your instructor, make sure the third party knows of your arrangement, agrees to it, and is properly insured for it.
4. Will the proper facilities be available? If, for example, you are going to jump, will there be rails and fences? If you are learning dressage, will there be a ring?
5. Whose horse will you ride? If yours, make sure the instructor knows what kind of horse he is and how much schooling he has had.

Before you begin your lessons, make sure all your questions are answered clearly. Never be intimidated. If there is anything you don't understand or don't like, say so. Successful schooling requires an honest and open relationship between a student and his teacher. Unless *your* teacher is someone you trust and respect, you will never act without questioning his advice. And, under such circumstances, you will never be safe in the saddle.

RIDING LESSONS FOR CHILDREN

Children should be taught to ride for two reasons: to encourage their interest in horses and to develop their prowess in a sport that is pleasurable and healthy. They should not be taught to ride so they can bolster their parents' egos with a roomful of ribbons.

This does not mean that children who enjoy competing should not do so, or that parents who take genuine pleasure in their children's activities and accomplishments should be denigrated. However, there is a tremendous difference between parents who are interested in their children and parents who are interested only in winning competitions. The latter have created one of the biggest problems in riding today. Constantly pressuring their children, pushing them too hard too soon, they pervert all the ideals of horsemanship. In the quest for ribbons, pleasure, camaraderie, sportsmanship all disappear. The show-ring becomes a battleground. Saddest of all, the children wind up turning their backs on a sport that could have given them great joy and satisfaction. To make sure your child is not among the casualties, *please* remember the following:

1. All children are made differently. Some are natural riders; others lack balance and coordination and must work twice as hard to get to the same point. The important thing is that every child be allowed to progress at his own rate. Any parent who pushes a child beyond his limits, speeds up his training, or demands that he compete before he is ready to do so not only exposes him to physical danger but damages him psychologically as well.

2. As a parent, it is your responsibility to find your child the right kind of instructor: one who is patient and understanding, one who will respect the child's fears, build his confidence, and never sacrifice his ego on the altar of achievement.

   However, once lessons have begun, it is important for the child's safety that he and the teacher develop a good, strong relationship. This means that you must adapt a hands-off policy—that you must not inject yourself into the lessons, make critical comments, or do anything to undermine the teacher's authority. If accidents are to be averted, the child must learn to follow the teacher's instructions without question or delay, and he can do this only if his teacher's voice is clear and uninterrupted.

3. Never measure your child's success by the number of ribbons he wins. True horsemanship has little to do with the show-ring. A child of average ability who loves horses and is dedicated to their welfare, is a far better horseman than the champion rider who lacks sympathy for his mount and has no respect for his feelings.

4-H CLUBS AND PONY CLUBS

Young riders throughout the country have access to two invaluable sources of instruction and information: the 4-H Club and the United States Pony Club. Although different in structure and emphasis, both these organizations teach the principles of good horsemanship and are superb training grounds for any youngster seriously interested in increasing his skills and expanding his knowledge.

THE 4-H HORSE PROGRAM

In its own words, the 4-H Horse Project helps its members to:

1. Develop leadership, initiative, self-reliance, sportsmanship, and other desirable traits of character.
2. Experience the pride of owning a horse or pony and being responsible for its management.

3. Develop an appreciation of horseback riding as a healthy and wholesome form of recreation.
4. Learn skill in horsemanship and an understanding of the business of breeding, raising, and training horses.
5. Increase knowledge of safety precautions to prevent injury to themselves, others, and their mount.
6. Promote greater love for animals and a humane attitude toward them.
7. To be better prepared for citizenship responsibilities through working in groups and supporting community horse projects and activities.

To be eligible, a boy or girl must be between ten and nineteen years of age and must own or manage a pony, horse, or foal. However, youngsters who do not own their own mounts should check this rule with their local 4-H chapter, since some clubs now buy or lease horses and divide the maintenance costs among their members. The 4-H Club has no membership fee.

Classes and instruction are given in horse care and management (i.e., grooming, feeding, shoeing, catching, tying, leading), training, care of equipment, horse psychology, and safety and first aid. Field trips, horse shows, trail rides, games on horseback, and community projects are among the major activities offered by the 4-H program.

To join, call your local Cooperative Extension (virtually every county in the United States has one), and ask for the name and address of the club nearest you. The Extension's telephone number is listed in the directory under United States Government, Department of Agriculture. Occasionally a 4-H Club will be listed in the Yellow Pages under Youth Organizations.

THE UNITED STATES PONY CLUB

The ideal of the Pony Club is to produce a happy and confident child on a happy and confident horse. It aims to teach and encourage riding and horse-oriented sports, instill a sense of sportsmanship and team spirit in young riders, and promote the welfare of the horse through proper care and understanding.

Boys and girls sixteen years of age and under are eligible. Although there is no minimum age requirement, the prospective member must be able to ride by himself, without the physical support of another person.

Although the word *pony* is used in the club's title, the member's mount can be either a horse or a pony. If a member does not own a horse, the club will arrange to have him borrow or lease one at a nominal cost.

The membership fee is $6.00 per year.

The Club offers instruction in riding and stable management, as well as instruction and team competition in combined training (dressage, cross-country, and stadium jumping), tetrathlon (a four-part event that consists of running, swimming, riding, and shooting air and CO_2 pistols), trail riding, polo, and mounted games.

For the name and address of the U.S. Pony Club nearest you, contact the Club's main headquarters at

> 303 South High Street
> West Chester, Pennsylvania 19380
> Telephone: (215) 436-0330

RIDING CAMP

In this age of specialization, selecting the right riding camp can be as difficult as buying the right horse. The choices are so numerous and the variety so great, that unless you know exactly what you are looking for, you are liable to get more—or less— than you bargained for. To make sure you find the proper niche and do not get involved in a program that is too advanced or too basic, learn to ask questions that will yield specific information about the camp you are considering.

WHAT TYPE OF CAMP IS IT?

Is it predominantly a riding camp, or is it a traditional camp that makes riding available to those who want it? In either case, which is taught, English or Western riding?

If the camp is predominantly a riding camp, how many hours a day are spent on horseback? What type of instruction is offered—jumping, cross-country, dressage, barrel racing? What is taught besides riding—horse care, first aid, etc.? Is the curriculum compulsory for all campers, or can each camper choose his own program?

Do the campers care for their own horses, or does the camp provide stable personnel? If horse care is left to the campers, exactly which duties are they expected to perform?

What activities are available besides riding—swimming, boating, water-skiing, tennis, archery, crafts? Is there an extra charge for these activities?

Are outside trips taken, to movies, horse shows, neighboring stables, towns?

VITAL STATISTICS

How many years has the camp been in existence?

Who are the instructors? What is their background?

What is the teacher-student ratio? What is the maximum number of students allowed in each class?

What kind of facilities are available for riding and schooling? Is there an indoor ring for use in inclement weather?

How many horses does the camp maintain *on its premises?* What kind of horses are they? Do campers get a chance to ride several different horses, or only one?

How many campers does the camp enroll? How old are they? Girls? Boys? Do they need any special qualifications? Will each camper be tested and classed according to his abilities, or will all campers be lumped together, regardless of experience?

COSTS

What is the price of the camp? Exactly what does this cover? Are there any extra charges? Are there any optional programs?

Can the camper bring his own horse? Is there a boarding fee? Insurance fee? Does the horse need a health certificate?

While the answers to these questions cannot convey the atmosphere of the camp or tell you how well it is run, they will at least narrow down the field of candidates and save you from a situation that is at odds with your training, experience, and expectations.

RIDING CAMPS AND THE LAW

When a youngster enrolls in a riding camp, the owner of the camp is under obligation to provide him with a safe and reliable horse and to see that a competent instructor accompanies him on his rides. Only if the owner is derelict in his duty—if he provides the youngster with a horse that is known to be dangerous, allows him to ride without proper supervision, or is otherwise negligent—can he be held legally responsible for any accidental injury the youngster incurs.

FIRST AID FOR THE HORSE AND RIDER

When accident occurs or sudden illness strikes, emergency treatment may be vitally needed. In such instances, time becomes very precious. A few minutes can make the difference between life and death, between minor injury and serious impairment. For this reason, and because medical help is not always readily available, every rider and every horseowner should have a working knowledge of first aid. While it cannot substitute for professional care, it *can* play a vital part in the patient's recovery and help keep him safe until the doctor arrives.

FIRST-AID KIT FOR THE HORSE

To administer proper treatment, you will need:

- Thermometer
- Pair of scissors
- Boric acid
- Disinfectant
- Petroleum jelly
- Antiseptic
- Cotton wool
- Various-sized adhesive bandages
- Race bandages
- Sterile gauze squares

Be sure to store these materials in a dry, clean, conveniently placed cabinet and replace any item that is worn out or used up.

HOW TO TREAT A HORSE'S WOUNDS

CUTS, TEARS, AND LACERATIONS

Stop the bleeding as quickly as possible. If bleeding is due to a leg injury, wrap a clean pressure bandage around the affected area. Extend it above and below the wound and make sure pressure is distributed evenly in all directions. If a piece of skin is hanging loose, place it in its proper position and include it in the bandage.

Bandages prevent swelling and reduce the chance of infection. Leave them on until the danger is past or until the vet arrives. Removing them prematurely can induce further bleeding. Note the use of a pressure bandage rather than a tourniquet. The latter can cause swelling and distress and should not be applied.

If bleeding is due to a head or body injury, bandaging will not be possible. In this instance, apply pressure directly to the wound by holding a clean cloth or towel over it and pressing down as hard as you can.

Clean a wound whenever possible. If bleeding is excessive,

don't waste time—stop it immediately. However, if your horse is not losing too much blood or if he is not overexcited, make every effort to clean out a wound before you bandage it. Wounds that do not bleed and wounds that are no longer bleeding when discovered, should also be cleaned. Use either plain soap and warm water, or a gentle stream of water from the hose. When bathing, never use a sponge, since it will always contain germs.

Cover up large holes. Deep wounds of the abdomen and chest require special handling to prevent the intestines from being exposed and expelled and to prevent outside air from entering the lungs. If there is a real danger of either, a pressure bandage must be applied directly to the wound. To keep it from slipping, wrap it completely around the abdomen or chest, up over the withers, and through the front legs.

PUNCTURE WOUNDS

When nails, sticks, thorns, or bits of metal or glass penetrate the skin, the resulting wound is often deceptive. Though small and innocent-looking, it can go very deep and cause serious infection. Always have it treated by a vet to prevent tetanus. If necessary, in the meantime, apply pressure to stop the bleeding. If the offending object is lodged in the foot and seems likely to be driven in further, remove it immediately, pour iodine into the gap, and plug it up with cotton. If there is no chance of further penetration, leave the object where it is until the vet can examine the wound.

BRUISES AND SPRAINS

Injuries caused by falls, kicks, or blows that *do not* break the skin are best treated with cold water to relieve pain and prevent swelling. Use running water from a hose, or else apply ice packs or cold water bandages as long as necessary. If you run water directly onto a horse's leg, do so gently. Start at his hoof to get him used to the idea, then gradually work your way up to the injured area.

EYE INJURIES

These are best handled by a veterinarian and should not be treated by the layman. However, if there is a foreign object in the eye that you can remove easily, do so. Otherwise, stable the horse in a darkened area and try to keep him from rubbing the injury.

FRACTURES

Your horse's survival may well depend on the way you treat a break in his legs. Begin by applying a pressure bandage, exactly as you would for an open wound. Then wrap a large pillow around the leg to make a splint, and fasten it as tightly as possible with bandages or tape. Again using bandages or tape, tie a stick (any type of handle or rod will do) to each side of the pillow for support. Try to keep the horse quiet and get professional help as fast as you can.

SADDLE SORES

Apply cold water or cold packs to reduce swelling and try to prevent scabs from forming. (Having them rubbed off is painful to the horse and starts the cycle all over again.) Keep off the horse until his back heals, then check to make sure his saddle fits properly. Don't use pads that harden or grow crusty and, if you use a foam rubber pad, put a blanket under it so that it does not heat up and burn the horse's back.

BURNS

Serious burns should be bathed with cool water, then covered with bandages to keep out contaminants. If the burn extends over a wide area, cover the horse with a clean sheet soaked in baking soda solution. Do not use antiseptics but see that the horse gets plenty of water to drink if he exhibits any signs of shock.

In the case of rope burns, clean the wound, apply medicated ointment and bandage.

SNAKE BITES

A horse in the pasture or on the trail will often lean down to examine a snake and get himself bitten on the nose. Swelling begins, followed by difficulty in breathing and danger of suffocation. To keep the air passages clear, hold the horse's nostrils open with your hands. Apply cold water to reduce swelling, and if, after a reasonable amount of time, it does not subside, puncture the skin around the bite with a sterilized knife.

COLIC

This is an abdominal upset that produces mild or severe pain, depending on the source of contamination (see Chapter 5). The affected horse will paw the ground and keep looking around at his flanks. Often he will kick at his belly or roll on the ground in an effort to ease his discomfort. Do not let him roll. Walk him until the pain subsides. If there is no letup within an hour, send for the vet.

LAMENESS

To prevent permanent damage to the horse, all foot problems should receive immediate attention. Begin by locating the trouble spot.

Has the horse cast a shoe?

Is there a stone in his foot?

Is there a wound? If so, pain, heat, and swelling should lead you to it.

Is there a foul odor? Thrush, an inflammation of the frog, will produce one. The foot should be washed with disinfectant, treated with antiseptic, and kept covered. The horse should be assured of dry, clean bedding.

Are the hooves dry and brittle? If they split, the horse will be lame. Dress them with oil (linseed or Neats-foot), pack them in wet clay, and keep the ground wet around the horse's water trough or bucket.

Are the feet inflamed? Have the horse stand on soft, muddy ground while you bathe them with cold water. Keep him off hard surfaces, and provide deep, heavy bedding.

FIRST-AID DO'S AND DON'TS

Don't judge the severity of an injury by its size. Large gaping wounds often heal faster and turn out to be less serious than small, innocent-looking ones that affect vital nerves and organs.

Don't treat any wound or illness with a medication or drug that has not been specifically prescribed for it by your veterinarian. Unauthorized tranquilizers are particularly dangerous. If a horse is close to shock, further relaxation of his lungs and heart can push him over the edge. Also, tranquilizers dull the senses. An injured horse who feels no pain may go on to do himself further injury.

Always choose your materials carefully. Use only dressings and medications that you know to be sterile. Never use safety pins. Never use bandages that will come apart or stick to the wound. When applying wet bandages, never use fabric that will shrink or tighten as it dries.

Always take care when approaching the scene of an accident. In your eagerness to help your horse, don't overlook dangers to yourself. This is particularly important in cases of electrical shock. Before you touch the victim, make sure he is free of the wire that downed him. If he isn't, his body is conducting electricity and will electrocute or shock on contact. Water, too, is a powerful conductor of electricity. It can convey the current of a live wire as far as thirty feet. If it is present in any form (puddles, rain) near the accident, *stay away*. Call the local fire department or electric company for help.

When caring for a sick or wounded horse, handle him gently and try to make him comfortable without too much fuss. Keep his bedding clean, and don't create extra dust by sweeping it or shaking it up. Change his water several times a day, and make sure he has plenty of it, particularly if he is feverish. Keep him out of drafts and direct sunlight, but don't cut down on his fresh air supply. Never overheat him with too many blankets. Check him frequently for sweating. If he is bandaged, make sure the bandages are not too tight. Change the dressing every day, and watch out for swelling. The amount of exercise and grooming he receives will depend on the nature of his disability. Ask your vet to advise you.

FIRST-AID KIT FOR THE RIDER

Every stable should maintain two first-aid kits—one for horses and one for humans. The latter should contain:

- A pair of scissors
- Sterile gauze pads
- Vaseline gauze
- Adhesive tape
- Band-Aids
- Safety pins
- A roll of sterile gauze
- An antiseptic such as hydrogen peroxide, Merthiolate, or alcohol
- Several scarves, large handkerchiefs, or triangular bandages that can be made into slings
- Material that can be used for splinting, such as strips of wood or metal, rolled-up newspapers, or blanketing

ADMINISTERING AID TO AN ACCIDENT VICTIM

Aside from summoning a doctor or an ambulance, there are four ways you can help the victim of an accident:

1. Make sure he can breathe
2. Stop his bleeding
3. Treat him for shock
4. Splint any broken limbs

The first of these is the most important. A seriously injured person may stop breathing at any time and, if this happens, you must put aside whatever else you are doing and administer artificial respiration without delay.

HOW TO GIVE ARTIFICIAL RESPIRATION

To apply the mouth-to-mouth method, first clear the patient's mouth and throat of any material that could block the air passage to his lungs—debris, mucous, loose dentures. Then, tilt back his head, hold up his chin, and breathe into his mouth.

Prevent the air from escaping by pinching his nostrils and sealing his mouth with your own.

If you are treating an adult, blow fifteen *deep* breaths per minute. If you are treating a small child, *cover both his nose and his mouth* with your mouth and blow twenty to twenty-five *shallow* breaths per minute. The patient's chest should rise each time you blow. If it doesn't, it may be that he has a blocked air passage or that the air is going to his stomach instead of to his lungs. Look deep into his mouth to see if there is any more debris that needs to be removed, and if there isn't, try tilting his head back further when you blow.

If proper mouth contact is impossible for any reason—if, for instance, the patient has sustained a bad mouth injury or there is some obstruction there that cannot be removed—apply mouth-to-nose resuscitation instead. This is done by closing the patient's mouth with your fingers and breathing into his nose.

Note: Most communities today offer free instruction in the new heart resuscitation techniques. For information, call your local Red Cross or Volunteer Ambulance Corps.

HOW TO STOP BLEEDING

No adult can lose more than a quart of blood (one pint for children) without suffering grave consequences. All severe bleeding must be checked immediately, particularly arterial bleeding, which is extremely rapid and will quickly bring a patient to the danger point.

Place a piece of sterile gauze directly on top of the wound and press down until the bleeding stops or slows. As you press, try to close the wound by gathering in all its edges. If the bleeding is arterial, blood will gush out in spurts and you will need to work very fast, applying stronger pressure than usual. Venous bleeding is slower, steadier, and easier to control.

If sterile gauze is not available, use the cleanest material you have on hand—a fresh handkerchief, a shirt, a strip of sheeting, etc.—and make sure it is large enough to cover the entire wound. When bleeding is especially severe, you may have to send an assistant for the material while you apply pressure with your bare hand. In this case, the risk of the patient bleeding to death is greater than the risk of infection.

Caution: Never apply a tourniquet to stop bleeding. Though once a popular method of control, it is now known to cause gangrene and loss of limbs and is used only when there is no other hope of saving the patient's life.

When applying direct pressure, make sure you apply it evenly to all parts of the wound. Pressing one area harder than another will keep the blood flowing.

When you have stopped the bleeding, cover the gauze (or other material) with a bandage. The bandage need not be sterile but should be large enough to cover the entire wound and snug enough to stay in place.

Caution: Leave the gauze in place when applying the bandage. Though it may be soaked through with blood, attempts to remove it may reactivate the bleeding.

Treat the patient for shock. If the wound is situated on an arm or a leg, elevate it on a pillow. Check the bandage frequently, to make sure swelling has not tightened it. If circulation is impaired, loosen it immediately.

Note: Tetanus bacteria are particularly prevalent in stables, barns, and other areas where horses live and graze. If you ride a horse, handle a horse, or work with a horse in any capacity, avoid infection by getting a tetanus shot.

HOW TO TREAT SHOCK

All severe injuries can produce a physical condition known as shock. This means that certain parts of the body lack sufficient blood to function properly and the heart must work hard to repair the deficit. As it does so, the patient exhibits a variety of symptoms: weak, but rapid, pulse; shallow, irregular breathing; pale, cold, clammy skin; dull or vacant expression; nausea; dizziness; and, often, unconsciousness.

In some cases, the patient looks perfectly normal, then suddenly collapses. The point here is that every person who sustains a deep wound, a broken bone, or a substantial blood loss, should be treated for shock even if the symptoms have not yet appeared. Strange as it may seem, the condition can prove fatal even though the injury that precipitated it was not substantial enough to kill.

To treat shock:

1. Have the patient lie down.
2. Implement the flow of blood to his head and heart by keeping his legs elevated. However, if he has sustained a head or chest injury or is not breathing well, elevate his head and chest, rather than his legs.
3. Place a blanket under him to prevent chill. If the day is cool, place a blanket *over* him as well. The idea is to provide warmth so the body can repair itself. *Caution:* Don't overheat the patient. Perspiration will have a detrimental rather than beneficial effect on his recovery.

HOW TO TREAT FRACTURES

Whenever a bone breaks, the resulting injury is called a fracture. The patient is rarely able to move the affected part of his body and usually suffers intense localized pain. Unless he is properly cared for *at the site of the accident*, he can be permanently disabled. For this reason, *any injury even vaguely resembling a fracture should be treated as if it actually were a fracture.* There are four important things to remember:

1. The patient is in dire need of professional medical help. Summon an ambulance or a doctor immediately.
2. Never move the patient until you have immobilized the affected area with a splint, sling, or other inhibiting device. However, if the patient has more to lose by remaining where he is, if, for example, he lies directly in the path of some oncoming danger, then you must move him.
3. Whenever you splint a fracture, be sure you do not cut off the patient's blood supply by making the ties too tight. Check the limb frequently for swelling.
4. Where fracture of any sort is involved, always treat the patient for shock.

Head Injury or Fractured Skull

The symptoms of head injury or fractured skull are: bleeding from the nose, mouth, or ears; slow breathing; noisy breathing; unconsciousness; paralysis; dizziness; flushed or hot face; nausea; and shock.

The patient may have a combination of symptoms or only one. Keep him lying down but, if his face is flushed, elevate his head and shoulders slightly. If he is unconscious, roll him over on his side to prevent him from swallowing his tongue. With your fingers, clear his mouth and throat of any material—earth, mucous, foreign objects—that could block the air passage to his lungs. If he is not breathing, place him on his back, loosen his collar and belt, and begin artificial respiration at once.

Broken Neck

If you suspect a fracture of the neck, do not try to alter the position of the patient's head, neck, and shoulders. Keep him flat on his back until the doctor arrives, and immobilize his head by placing a firm object on either side of it. Never place his head on a pillow. If you must move him, have an assistant hold his head still so his neck does not bend.

Back Injury or Broken Back

A fallen rider complaining of an injured back should not be moved until the doctor arrives. If his back is fractured, the broken bones can cut the spinal cord and cause paralysis or death. However, if he lies in the path of danger and absolutely must be moved, position yourself behind his head and crouch down as close to the ground as you possibly can. Then, grab him under the arms and, with a *slow, steady* movement, pull him to safety. If you prefer, you may position yourself at his feet instead of at his head and pull him by the ankles. *Never* try to pick him up by his head and feet. And never twist his head or allow it to fall forward.

Broken Rib

A rider who sustains a chest injury and feels sharp pain whenever he moves, coughs, or breathes deeply is probably suffering from a broken rib. If his pain is unusually severe, you can relieve it by strapping his chest above and below the fracture (the point of pain) with wide strips of adhesive tape. The straps should start at the middle of his chest, pass over the fracture, and end at the middle of his back, at the spine.

Broken Collarbone

This is the most common of all riding injuries and can be identified by a drooping shoulder and a pain in the arm on the affected side. Have the rider sit up and support the aching arm under the elbow, while you place it in a sling and then bind it to his chest. Never include his fingers in the sling.

For this operation, you will need two separate bandages: a triangular one for the sling and a plain one for the binding. If neither is available, use a scarf, necktie, large handkerchief, or stock tie.

Broken Leg

Whenever fracture exists or is even thought to exist, the leg must be splinted before the rider can be moved. Lay him down and keep him as warm as possible. (Chances are he is also suffering from shock and must be treated for this as well.) Make a splint out of any rigid material you have on hand—a piece of wood or metal padded with cloth, an umbrella, a tightly rolled newspaper, even a blanket or a pillow. Extend the splint beyond the joints above and below the fracture, then tie it to the leg with bandages or strips of cloth. Never try to remove the rider's boot. Elevate the leg above the level of the heart, and check the ties frequently to be sure they are not tight enough to cause swelling or impair circulation.

If the injury is an open (or compound) fracture, a fracture accompanied by an open wound or laceration, you will have to apply direct pressure to stop any *serious* bleeding. If the bleeding is arterial, apply pressure above the site of the wound, between the wound and the body. If the bleeding is venous, apply pressure between the wound and the extremity. If the rider's boot prevents you from reaching a pressure point, *cut* it away—pulling it off will cause the patient excruciating pain. When the bleeding has stopped, cover the wound with a clean handkerchief, towel, or sheet to prevent infection.

Broken Arm

The treatment here is very much the same as it is for a broken collarbone. Jostling the arm as little as possible, place it in a sling and bind it to the patient's chest. Offset the effects of shock by keeping him warm.

HOW TO TREAT SPRAINS

When an ankle, wrist, knee, or any other joint of the body is wrenched without actually being dislocated and the tissue around the joint is damaged, the injury is called a sprain. Sprains should be bathed in cold water (to reduce swelling), bandaged (for support), and then elevated. Severe sprains should be splinted, just in case the force of the accident also fractured a bone.

TREATING OTHER SPECIFIC INJURIES

Chest Wounds

A hole in the chest caused by a blow or a penetrating object can sometimes open the lungs to the outside air. As the air passes in and out of the wound, you may hear a hissing noise or see froth or bubbles. To close the hole, place your hands on either side of it and push it together when the patient exhales. Apply a dressing made of sterile vaseline gauze (only vaseline gauze will make the dressing airtight), and keep it in place with a firm bandage. Treat the patient for shock, but don't elevate his feet unless you are sure he has no problem breathing.

Puncture Wounds

These are particularly prone to tetanus infection and should be squeezed gently to encourage bleeding. After being thoroughly cleansed, they should be covered loosely with a sterile dressing and treated by a physician.

Minor Wounds

Once bleeding is under control, all minor wounds should be treated to prevent infection. Using a sterile gauze pad, not your fingers, wash the affected area gently but thoroughly with soap and water or plain water. Cover it with a sterile dressing, and fasten the dressing with strips of adhesive or a bandage. Never wash any wound which has bled excessively.

Wounds Inflicted by Horses

If a horse kicks you, just about the only thing you can do is bathe the area with cold running water to relieve pain. For bites, again, apply cold water to relieve pain and wash away germs. If the skin is broken, treat like all other open wounds and have the doctor check for infection. If a horse steps on you and you have proper footwear, you will usually suffer some pain but no other damage. A barefoot rider, or one wearing soft shoes, may sustain serious injury and should be seen by a doctor.

APPENDIX

THE HORSEMAN'S DIRECTORY

The following are the names and addresses of organizations that offer information, instruction, and assistance to riders and horseowners throughout the United States.

American Dressage Institute
249 Round Hill Road
Greenwich, Connecticut 06830

American Horse Council
Suite 300
1700 K Street, N.W.
Washington, D.C. 20006

American Farriers Association
P.O. Box 695
Albuquerque, New Mexico 87103

American Horse Shows Association
598 Madison Avenue
New York, New York 10022

American Hunter and Jumper
Horse Association
Box 1174
Fort Wayne, Indiana 46801

Horseman's Benevolent and
Protective Association
600 Executive Boulevard
Rockville, Maryland 20852

Humane Society of the United
States
2100 L Street, N.W.
Washington, D.C. 20037

National Fire Protection Association
470 Atlantic Avenue
Boston, Massachusetts 02110

This association will provide
literature on fire safety for stables,
barns, and farms.

National 4-H Service Committee
150 North Wacker Drive
Chicago, Illinois 60606

National Little Britches Rodeo
Association
2160 South Holly
Suite 105
Denver, Colorado 80222

National Trails Council
53 West Jackson Boulevard
Chicago, Illinois 60604

New Hampshire Horse and Trail
Association
322 North Adams Street
Manchester, New Hampshire 03104

North American Riding For The
Handicapped Association
Box 100
Ashburn, Virginia 22001

Headquarters of a national
organization that helps the
physically and emotionally
handicapped develop better muscle
control through horseback riding.
The exercise programs are
monitored by a physician and a
physical therapist and are free to all
participants. The association will be
happy to provide you with the
name of a therapy center in your
area.

North American Trail Ride
Conference
1995 Day Road
Gilroy, California 95020

Professional Horsemen's
Association of America
Route 1
Midland, Georgia 31820

United States Animal Health
Association
1444 East Main Street
Richmond, Virginia 23219

United States Combined Training
Association
1 Winthrop Square
Boston, Massachusetts 02110

United States Dressage Federation
Inc.
Box 80668
Lincoln, Nebraska 68501

United States Equestrian Team Inc.
Gladstone, New Jersey 07934

United States Government
Department of Agriculture
Cooperative Extension Service

Information, instruction, and assistance in all areas of Horse Care, Stable Management and Construction, Pasturing. Will also provide the names of all local 4-H Clubs. The address will be found in your local telephone directory.

United States Polo Association
1301 West 22nd Street
Suite 706
Oak Brook, Illinois 60521

United States Pony Club
303 South High Street
West Chester, Pennsylvania 19380

This is the national headquarters. Their telephone number, which you can call to find out the location of the Pony Club closest to you, is (215) 436-0300.

STATE HORSE COUNCILS

Alaska State Horsemen, Inc.
P.O. Box 4-012
Anchorage, Alaska 99509

Arizona State Horsemen's
Association
5001 East Washington
Suite 128
Phoenix, Arizona 85034

California Horse Council
224 East Olive
Burbank, California 91502

Colorado Horsemen's Council
15504 West 52nd Street
Arvada, Colorado 80002

Connecticut Horse Council
Holines Road
East Lyme, Connecticut 06333

Florida Horse Council
Room 415
Mayo Building
Tallahassee, Florida 32301

Georgia Horse Council
2552 Habersham Road, N.W.
Atlanta, Georgia 30305

Iowa Horse Council
Route 1
North Liberty, Iowa 52317

Massachusetts Horsemen's Council,
Inc.
91 Grove Street
Box 117
Upton, Massachusetts 01568

Minnesota Horse Council
P.O. Box 292
Long Lake, Minnesota 55356

Michigan Horse Council
P.O. Box 12074
Lansing, Michigan 48902

Mississippi Horse Council
700 Main Street
Columbia, Mississippi 39429

Missouri Horse and Mule Council
Box 101
Lynn Creek, Missouri 65052

Nevada State Horsemen's
Association
1545 West Wells Avenue
Reno, Nevada 89502

New England Horsemen's Council,
Inc.
327 Parker Street
East Longmeadows, Massachusetts
01028

New Jersey Horse Council
310 West State Street
Trenton, New Jersey 08618

New Mexico Horse Council
P.O. Box 543
Corrales, New Mexico 87048

North Carolina Horse Club
Box 308
Zebulon, North Carolina 27597

Ohio Horsemen's Council
P.O. Box 302
Lebanon, Ohio 45036

Oklahoma Horsemen's Association
2525 Northwest Expressway
Oklahoma City, Oklahoma 73112

Pennsylvania Equine Council
324 Animal Industry Building
University Park, Pennsylvania
16802

South Carolina Horse Council
Extension Horse Specialist
Clemson University
Clemson, South Carolina 29631

Texas Horse Council
5314 Bingle Road
Houston, Texas 77018

Virginia Horse Council
P.O. Box 72
Riner, Virginia 24149

West Virginia Horse Council
West Virginia Department of
Agriculture
Charlestown, West Virginia 25305

Wisconsin State Horse Council
Route 2, Box 65
Brooklyn, Wisconsin 53521

INDEX